Praise for Gene Ludwig and *The Mismeasurement of America*

"In *The Mismeasurement of America*, Gene Ludwig and his team demonstrate that policymakers need to change the way we look at economic data to reflect the real experience of Americans in their daily lives. The insights in this book show us that if we challenge ourselves to think outside the box, we have the tools to restore the basic bargain of the American Dream."

—Hillary Rodham Clinton

"Gene Ludwig and his team reveal the true state of our economy, putting us back on the path to growth. Grounded in thoughtful research, *The Mismeasurement of America* cuts through to the truth and shows us how to make economic opportunity and fair play real for all."

—Glenn Hubbard, Russell L. Carson Professor of Finance and Economics, Columbia University, and former Chair of the President's Council of Economic Advisers

"For opportunity to be real for all Americans everywhere, we have to understand that reality. Today we don't. In *The Mismeasurement of America*, Gene Ludwig and his team show us how we can—and with that understanding, how we can create meaningful economic opportunity for all. With his signature thoughtful, research-driven approach, Ludwig gets to the heart of the economic anxiety so many Americans experience and what policymakers across the political spectrum are missing. A must-read for those who care about a better future for America."

—Deval Patrick, investor, business executive, lawyer, and former Governor of Massachusetts

"In case there were any doubts about the sinking economic well-being of middle- and low-income Americans, Gene Ludwig persuasively confirms it. In *The Mismeasurement of America*, Ludwig, deploying a forensic team of economic statistic experts, unflinchingly dissects our most commonly quoted statistics, like inflation and earnings, revealing them to be deficient in reflecting most Americans' economic experiences. With the characteristic clear-eyed perspective that readers saw in *The Vanishing American Dream* comes a call to tear off the blinders to the lived experiences of middle- and low-income Americans and do better in aligning our statistical measures with how life is lived."

—Sarah Bloom Raskin, former US Treasury Deputy Secretary

"In *The Mismeasurement of America*, Gene Ludwig describes how conventional measures of economic performance don't reveal the true state of the economy for many Americans. Ludwig critiques the measures we use and proposes new ways to capture central forces like inflation, which can be much higher for Americans who are struggling than the headline numbers suggest."

—Robert E. Rubin, Cochair Emeritus, Council on Foreign Relations, and former US Treasury Secretary

"Many books have detailed the lack of broadly shared prosperity in recent decades. This one is unique in suggesting that the problem is not just the failure to enact better policy, but flaws in our current data that provide a misleading picture of the well-being of middle- and low-income families. Especially innovative is the attempt to define a minimal quality of life that could be provided to all if there were more sharing of economic progress. Despite being about data, the book is also a readable and impassioned plea to restore the American Dream."

—Isabel Sawhill, Senior Fellow Emeritus at the Brookings Institution

"In Gene Ludwig's new book, he doesn't blame the bureaucracy for politicizing economic data. He reveals the more banal but insidious truth: The conception, collection, and publication of much of our economic data is deeply flawed. Misleading data leads to misguided economic decision-making, undermining the residual trust between the elected and the electorate."

—Kevin Warsh, former Governor of the Federal Reserve

The

Mismeasurement of America

The

Mismeasurement of America

How Outdated Government Statistics Mask the Economic Struggle of Everyday Americans

GENE LUDWIG

DISRUPTION
BOOKS
Washington, DC

Published by Disruption Books
Washington, DC
www.disruptionbooks.com
Copyright © 2025 The Ludwig Institute for Shared Economic Prosperity

Distributed by Disruption Books

For information about special discounts for bulk purchases, please
contact Disruption Books at info@disruptionbooks.com.

Cover images used under license from iStockphoto:
1467962165/kemalbas and 1477450771/Bim

Cover and book design by Sheila Parr

Library of Congress Cataloging-in-Publication Data available

Printed in the United States of America.

Print ISBN: 978-1-63331-134-3
eBook ISBN: 978-1-63331-135-0

First Edition

10 9 8 7 6 5 4 3 2

I dedicate this book to my amazing family, who are constant sources of inspiration: To my wonderful wife Carol; children Abigail, Elizabeth, and David; son-in-law Evan; granddaughter Evelyn; and brother Ken.

Contents

Acknowledgments

I want to acknowledge my talented collaborators on this book—most notably Philip Cornell, our exceptional chief economist, and Santiago Dassen and Shannon Meyer, our dedicated analysts, who provided invaluable expertise, along with Gina Simpson, the careful and creative head of our marketing and communications department, who played a crucial role in both editing this work and refining our graphics. Special thanks to Marc Dunkelman, Kathleen Goldstein, Louie Giacomini, and Brai Valerio-Esene for their editorial and research contributions. I am also grateful to Kris Pauls and the Disruption Books team for their unwavering support throughout this project.

The genesis of this book can be traced back to a Yale Law School symposium that brought together leading scholars, policymakers, and business leaders. This gathering, cohosted by Dean Heather Gerken, sparked the initial conversation that laid the foundation for this research. I am deeply indebted to the symposium participants, including Jacob Hacker, Jonathan Macey, Daniel Markovits, Zachary Liscow, Anika Singh Lemar, Robert Shiller, Oren Cass, Steven Pearlstein, Andrea Levere, Sarah Bloom Raskin, Larry Summers, Glenn Hubbard, Andrew Tisch, Mary Skafidas, Isabel Sawhill, Luke Bronin, Jay Shambaugh, Daryl Byrd, Mary Miller, Michael Moskow, Deval Patrick, Susan Krause Bell, and David Newville, for their invaluable insights and contributions.

Introduction

This book might seem, at first glance, somewhat arcane. After all, it is mostly an examination of economic statistics found in key US headlines. In fact, some might view such an exercise as not only arcane but also not worth their time. Why is scrutinizing oft-cited, government-headline statistics so important? Do they offer a reasonably accurate snapshot of America? Shockingly, this is not the case, particularly as these statistics portray the well-being of middle- and low-income Americans.

Importantly, then, this book addresses three core questions: First, what, if anything, is wrong with the picture of America painted by the prevailing figures? Second, what does a more accurate picture look like? And third, if the headline government economic statistics do inaccurately portray lower- and middle-income Americans, how can they be changed or supplemented to better reflect reality?

Alternatively, if viewing the book and its subject matter through a narrow lens, some will wonder whether its insights have the potential to have any real impact. Why should anyone put in the effort to do anything to correct rather academic misperceptions, however widespread? Is improving the focus of our economic measurements worth the effort? All fair questions.

In order to answer them, you need to understand a bit about my background. I was born in York, Pennsylvania, a small farming and industrial city at the edge of the quaint and beautiful Amish country, but I've worked most of my career in Washington, as a lawyer, as an economic policymaker, and perhaps most importantly, as a financial regulator, serving for several years as comptroller of the currency. Over the last decade or more, when I traveled back home to York, I noticed something of growing concern: Economic circumstances on the ground in Pennsylvania were increasingly askew from the narrative my peers in policymaking circles in Washington presumed to be true. Things in York weren't booming, as you might have presumed listening to roundtable discussions in the nation's capital. On the contrary. And so, I began to ask why that was.

After several years of making these observations, I formed a hypothesis: The economic statistics that form the basis of economic reality are giving policymakers inaccurate renderings of reality.

At first, that was just a notion—a hunch that I couldn't yet prove to be true. But I was determined to see my intuition through, and so I hired a crack team of young scholars and economists to work at what we termed the Ludwig Institute for Shared Economic Prosperity, or LISEP. Once these researchers were on board, I asked them to begin what became a forensic analysis with a crucial goal: to understand the roots of the chasm separating perception and reality. The pages that follow are a report arising from what we uncovered.

My hope is that after reading this book, you will come to conclusions mirroring my own and share my conviction about the critical importance of accurate government statistics, especially when it comes to understanding the economic reality for lower- and middle-income Americans, a group that comprises more than half of our fellow Americans. Examining this point is even more important because the data reveals just how tenuous the economic situation is for this large and financially vulnerable segment of our country.

My belief, after engaging in a multiyear study and writing this book, is that the headline statistics paint a far too rosy and fundamentally misleading picture of the economic realities faced by middle- and low-income Americans. Furthermore, I've come to conclude that giving policymakers and ordinary Americans a more accurate picture will lead to much improved policies and a better economic future for our nation. Understanding why this is true requires first confronting the depths of our current misperception. This book delves into this misperception and sheds light on the true reality.

Cynics will argue that whatever tweaks policymakers might make, even if they were to demonstrate a better understanding of reality, wouldn't have much effect. These cynics will claim that today's problems are born primarily from the unending battle, and sometimes stalemate, between the left and the right based on their different interpretations of economic events. I disagree.

I found something in the course of this research—a remarkable convergence of views across the political spectrum. While engaging, through presentations and discussions, with businesspeople, academics, policymakers, and activists of all stripes, my research team and I found broad agreement—regardless of political affiliation—on our inquiry method, approach, and conclusions. And the findings detailed in the pages that follow lead most people who read them to conclude that the government's headline-making economic statistics need revamping, largely in line with the approaches we suggest. Furthermore, there is widespread agreement that America needs to greatly expand and refine its efforts to improve the lives of middle- and lower-income Americans.

Beneath this agreement, however, is an ominous warning. As our team uncovered the flaws in the prevailing picture of America's economy—distortions drawn from the headline data—we concluded that the failure to paint a more accurate picture is leading us down a path to economic and societal unrest of considerable proportions. This is not hyperbole. Time and again, history is marked with moments when a government's failure to fully appreciate the realities faced by ordinary people prompted a crisis. Without *realizing* it, America may well be on the brink of such a moment.

We've seen this movie before—the one where those possessing the power and authority to head off an economic crisis are blind to its emergence. It's for this very reason that some of the most well-regarded market gurus and macroeconomists are frequently cynical, if not fatalistic, about the potential of prognostications to help policymakers keep economies on track.

I can't agree. There is no reason to throw up our hands. Quite often, the failure to take timely action is born not from intellectual helplessness but from failing to speak truth to power—particularly when "the emperor has no clothes" and when speaking out loudly carries personal risk.

Of course, it is not always a lack of courage that impedes truth-telling. At times, the data presented to policymakers is either incomplete or flawed in some material way. In those moments, it becomes much easier to accept common conventions. Historically, flaws in widely accepted economic statistics have impeded important decision-making. But all too often, those who could have done something were left unaware or, worse, willfully ignored the warning signs that contradicted the rosier numbers—to catastrophic effect.

In many cases, those who accept economic misrepresentations do so for reasons that are entirely benign: The data is too difficult to collect with sufficient regularity or precision. The samples aren't sufficiently comprehensive. Human nature favors expeditious, rosy analysis rather than the rigor required to glean accuracy, particularly when accurate numbers may be gloomy. But in other instances, the underlying cause is not so innocent: Data is mismeasured because powerful groups and institutions have little incentive—and frequently face disincentives—to correct the stilted figures.

The research presented in the following chapters has found that regardless of the *cause* of our failure to improve our economic measures, we are continually fooling ourselves—or being fooled—that the glass is half full. And the headline statistics paint a misleading picture of America. Furthermore, government statistics being off base is not a new story nor is it just an American story. Alas, humanity has seen this tale play out far too often.

The Great Depression and the economic crisis that led to the French Revolution are both cases in point. In the late eighteenth century, the oppressive economic situation facing the French people went unacknowledged for decades by the royal family. Much as the monarchy's finance minister might have tried to maintain a reliable and accurate accounting of the public purse, the French ruling class considered the truth about the nation's fiscal crisis to be nefarious—a threat both to their power and to their freedom to spend tax dollars lavishly on themselves.[1] With eyes askance and heads in the proverbial sand, they refused to acknowledge the economic reality, typified by Queen Marie Antoinette's likely apocryphal suggestion that, if the peasants were starving for want of bread, "let them eat cake!"[2] Of course, we know what happened not long thereafter: Marie Antoinette and many of her peers were guillotined, and the chaos born of the French Revolution wrought untold horrors on French citizens of every rank and station.

The same narrative arc applied a century and a half later as the Great Depression loomed. In both instances, economic data that *could* have set off alarm bells was available—more accurate figures that would have revealed the risks emerging *before* the stock market crashed and the subsequent depression hit—and this perspective might have prompted action that could have softened the blow, if not avoided the crisis altogether.[3] But the data was either confusing, confounded with other contrary data, or affirmatively hidden. And the effects were catastrophic.

The economic indicators that prevailed through the 1920s suggested that nearly all was right with the world: The national economy and underlying markets were growing. Employment was strong.[4] Few questioned the picture painted by figures variously released by both the government and private-sector analysts.[5] Indeed, among a number of similar stories from the time, one is particularly striking, showing how wrongheaded even notable experts can be when they do not have to confront the real data: Just two weeks before the stock market crash of October 1929, the celebrated economist

Irving Fisher declared that "stock prices have reached what looks like a permanently high plateau."[6]

But in hindsight, we know that the prevailing numbers were distortions.

Not everyone was bamboozled. The brilliant Supreme Court Justice Louis Brandeis couldn't help but raise questions. Brandeis could see how the rosy statistics being issued by President Calvin Coolidge's Labor Department did not square with the stories he'd heard from farmers around the country, many of whom were in economic trouble and laying off hired hands. This was March of 1928, half a year before Herbert Hoover would be elected president and more than eighteen months before the stock market crashed. Rural America's experience was entirely divergent from the narrative many in Washington were drawing from the government's unemployment figures. And Brandeis had come to suspect the reason for the disparity: The Labor Department was mismeasuring *who* was employed.[7] The arcana of economic statistics was working to catastrophic effect.

Well before President Woodrow Wilson had appointed him to the country's highest tribunal, Brandeis had begun worrying about what he termed the "regularity of income." Brandeis recognized that for many, if not most, working Americans, a job did not provide economic stability. On the contrary, most Americans had no guarantee their jobs would last from month to month or even week to week. Many people were mere "seasonal" employees—they were not "steady in [their] work," to use Brandeis's phrase.[8] But that nuance wasn't captured in the contemporary economic data or analysis, which suggested that a job was full-time and somewhat steady. To the contrary, like today, the definitions provided that someone who worked even part-time or seasonally was simply considered "employed," implying they were more steady in their work than was actually the case.[9] Many pundits of the time were blind to just how quickly the economy could unravel and take jobs away with it.[10]

In reality, the nation's economy was on the precipice of disaster, and circumstances had been trending down for the better part of a decade. After ramped-up production during World War I, the rural US economy was subsequently hampered by a dramatic postwar slack in demand and lower prices. And that had prompted a vicious cycle: Farmers had been incented to plant more to meet their debts, expanding the wedge between supply and demand, and driving prices further down.[11] By the late 1920s, farmhands were being turned out, and neither they nor their employers could pay their debts, many of which were owed to community banks. It wasn't until a glut of foreclosures began to pile up among lenders that the public began to lose confidence not just in the banking system but in the economy as a whole.[12]

The Great Depression, of course, would prove to be an economic catastrophe of unparalleled breadth and pain. Its effects remain infamous. Perhaps more notably, its causes have been the subject of unceasing examination, sparking debates about its roots, how policymakers might have reacted more effectively, and what, in the end, finally pulled the country out on the other side. But the economic establishment's failure to anticipate or prepare for the danger should be remembered most poignantly today for another reason: In its echo, we can recognize our own circumstances.

CR

The chapters that follow discuss the four key headline statistics on which many economic policy decisions hinge in the United States today and how these metrics create a distorted picture of our economic reality. Together, these pages warn that the tenor of today's economic debate reflects, in many ways, the same obliviousness that preceded previous upheavals.

Chapter 1 focuses on the unemployment statistics that the Bureau of Labor Statistics (BLS) touts monthly, revealing why the *true* rate of unemployment generally runs more than twenty percentage points higher. The divergence marks an echo of Justice Brandeis's worry in the 1920s: The BLS's numbers count workers as "employed" even if they *want* a full-time position but have settled for a part-time alternative—even one that accounts for as little as an hour per week. They are also counted as "employed" even if their full-time position pays a poverty wage, which is defined as earning less than $25,000 per year.[13]

Chapter 2 unpacks weekly earnings and, again, finds serious flaws in the prevailing statistics as announced. For example, the BLS numbers exclude part-time employees and the jobless who are seeking work—so weekly earnings include only those who have full-time jobs.[14] As a result, the prevailing measure shows an overstated wage rather than the reality for many middle- and low-income Americans, and it even appears to improve perversely during economic downturns because low-wage workers are disproportionately affected by layoffs.[15]

Chapter 3 delves into the prevailing measure of inflation and, more specifically, how price changes affect those with disparate incomes.

Here, the headline Consumer Price Index (CPI) obscures as much as it illuminates. By aggregating price changes of roughly eighty thousand goods and services rather than focusing on necessary items that eat up the wages of low- and moderate-income households—food, housing, and health care, for example[16]—the CPI distracts from the reality that median earnings have declined vis-à-vis ordinary expenses. In fact, prices for unavoidable expenses have risen about 35 percent *faster* than the CPI, leaving many households to struggle ever harder, year after year, to make ends meet.[17]

Chapter 4 answers what should be a simple and straightforward question: In light of gross domestic product (GDP) growth—widely adopted by economists, businesses, and the public at large as a measure of a nation's overall economic success—is it easier or more difficult for Americans to acquire what we term a "minimal quality of life"?[18] What we found was dispiriting: Notwithstanding the considerable growth in national economic wealth over the past twenty years, middle- and lower-income Americans continue to fall further behind those at the top. If middle- and lower-income American households are not able to share more broadly in economic growth, they may abandon altogether the hope of ever achieving the American Dream. And the potential consequences of that ensuing dissatisfaction are untold.

Taken together, these four chapters paint a picture of what life looks like for middle- and low-income Americans that is very different from what the average observer or even an analyst would glean from regularly touted headline statistics. Irrespective of whether you take issue with elements of our research, I hope that, first, you will come away from this book convinced that the current headline statistics should be supplemented or even replaced. We simply need a better way to understand what's actually happening in the economy—and absent major revisions, that will not be possible.

Second, we hope this book compels you to take seriously the picture our alternative indicators paint for middle- and lower-income Americans. Compared to their higher-income counterparts, people in these demographics are experiencing a significant decline in well-being. This translates into a growing sense of hardship, frustration, and a simmering resentment toward a system perceived as unfair.

The approach our team took in analyzing the data is somewhat fresh, and the conclusions are unquestionably stark. To me, however, they did not come entirely as a surprise.

Several years ago, I edited a book, *The Vanishing American Dream*, which was born from a Yale Law School symposium of well-regarded scholars, businesspeople, activists, and politicians from various political perspectives.[19] Everyone around the table shared much the same concern about the fate of America's middle- and lower-income demographic groups. Anecdotal evidence, reflected in a number of distinguished books and reports published around the same time, suggested that something was seriously amiss. We were awash with reports of suicides, spikes in crime, neighborhoods in decline, job scarcity, and poor education—all harbingers of unrest.

The totality of evidence at the time reflected my experience while tracking the evolution of York, Pennsylvania. During my youth, York had been one of the most prosperous small cities in America. In more recent years, the prevailing statistics led many living in more cosmopolitan corners of the country to presume that economies like York's were holding their own or even improving. But that was not my impression upon returning to visit my hometown. The situation in York has echoes of Justice Brandeis's comment before the Great Depression: Despite the conclusions many were drawing from the statistics, the decline was obvious and unmistakable. And, as Brandeis experienced, the discordancy makes it hard to get one's mind around the publicized figures.

This book is the result of the multiyear endeavor inspired by the concern that ensued from these discussions and observations. Had the headline numbers been right, and was the anecdotal evidence an artifact of past impressions? That would have been a welcome conclusion. But lamentably, as you will read, reality is more accurately rendered by what people have seen and heard for themselves. As in Brandeis's experience, it is the numbers that have been misleading.

I urge you to dig in and come to your own conclusions. Perhaps you will uncover a silver lining, a reason to interpret the data in a way that doesn't elicit so much gloom. But if you share my interpretation—namely, to quote William Shakespeare, that "something is rotten in the state of Denmark"—I hope you will carefully consider our conclusions and suggestions at the end of this book as pathways out of the current swamp. As the evidence sparks new ideas—strategies that might help middle- and working-class Americans feel once again that they *can* achieve the American Dream—I hope you will share your thoughts and feedback with us as we consider another multiyear study to plot, in greater detail, a path toward earnestly shared prosperity.

Chapter 1

True Rate of Unemployment

HOUSTON, WE HAVE A PROBLEM

What might the employment statistics from one US city reveal about the economic health of the nation as a whole? In asking this question, the Ludwig Institute for Shared Economic Prosperity focused on Houston, Texas—which, of course, is not a microcosm of the whole country. But the unemployment rate in Houston is certainly relevant because the region might reflect what is happening elsewhere in the United States. At the very least, Houston could offer lessons about improving the employment outcomes for Hispanic populations elsewhere in America.

At first glance, then, these economic statistics that help frame our understanding of the economy would seem to quiet the concerns of those worried about inequality in metropolitan Houston and perhaps America in its entirety.

Conventional wisdom has it that the Houston area's Hispanic residents—a demographic that comprises roughly 40 percent of the population[1]—suffer from a much higher prevalence of unemployment than does the city's general population, in large part due to prejudice and the legacy of discrimination.[2] Moreover, many analysts, also in line with conventional wisdom, would likely presume that Hispanic *women* are at a particular disadvantage. And all that would make some sense: A population that skews poorer, less educated, and more likely to be first-generation American citizens would presumably find it harder to land a job, at least when compared to their wealthier, more established, White neighbors.[3] But recent headline statistics generated by the federal government—the Bureau of Labor Statistics, to be exact—would suggest, much to most outsiders' surprise, that the conventional wisdom is wrong.

According to the prevailing BLS headline unemployment indicator (known as "the U-3"), Hispanic women in the Houston area are not actually that far behind the rest of Houston.[4] In 2023, the difference between the Houston Hispanic women's unemployment rate and the overall Houston unemployment rate was a mere one-tenth of a percentage point: 5.0 percent unemployment for Houston Hispanic women compared with 4.9 percent for Houston residents overall.[5] Houston, of course, is not a microcosm of the whole country. But this surprisingly good unemployment news is certainly welcome because the region, with its high Hispanic population, might reflect what is happening elsewhere in the United States or, at the very least, offer lessons about improving the employment outcomes for Hispanic populations elsewhere. The Houston metropolitan region provides a sufficiently robust case study to draw some broader conclusions. And the conclusions almost any observer would draw from the indicators published by the BLS would appear to be a just cause for optimism.

Here's what seems like even better news: This miniscule divergence in Houston's unemployment rates isn't some once-in-a-blue-moon anomaly. At least in recent years, it appears to be the normal state of affairs. Since 2000, with a brief exception during the Covid-19 pandemic, the two headline unemployment figures—the U-3 for Houston's Hispanic women and the U-3 for Houston as a whole—tracked basically the same arc. At several moments, Hispanic female unemployment was actually *below* the figure for the overall Houston population.

If nothing else, this small slice of economic data would seem to support the notion that the American Dream is, far from gasping for breath, alive and well. If Hispanic women in Houston are keeping pace with the region's broader population—if a community presumed to be stuck on the bottom rungs of the economic ladder is actually holding its own—who could reasonably complain that they are systemically hampered? Or that they need an extra boost? Or that prejudice, which many now accept as a barrier that runs deep in American society, is having a material effect on their well-being? Here is evidence, it would seem, that the great promise of American prosperity remains intact—that those who come here from abroad or are born into tough circumstances can succeed no matter their race, creed, color, or gender.

Unfortunately, while the U-3 numbers quoted above are accurate given the data collected and the definition used, they are, alas, misleading. Yes, the numbers that underlie the U-3 are accurate and, yes, the government produces its ultimate calculation with the same care and fidelity it has applied since the definition of "unemployment" came into use in the 1930s.[6] But there is a fly in the ointment, a worm in the apple. The all-important filter through which the numbers are

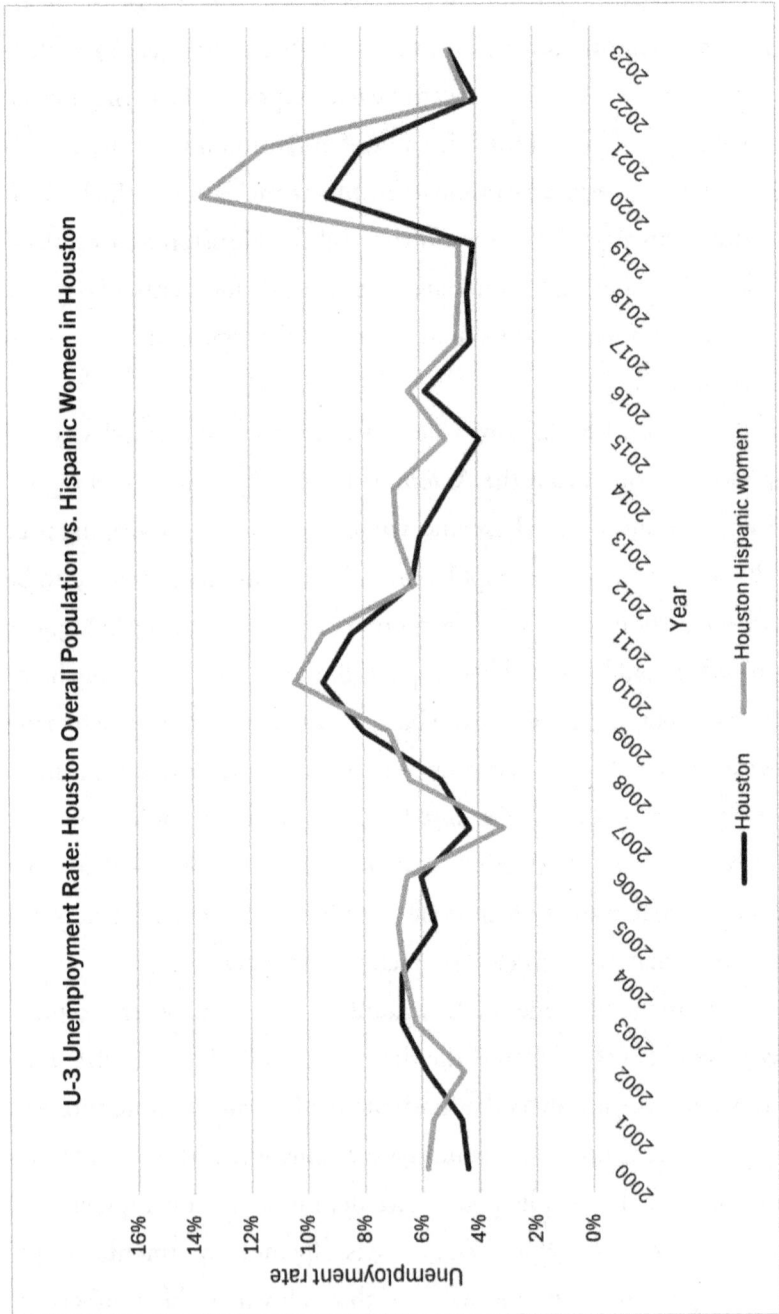

U-3 Unemployment Rate: Houston Overall Population vs. Hispanic Women in Houston

run—the 1930s definition of what counts as "unemployed"—is, in our twenty-first-century world, badly off the mark.

Here's the rub: If someone is looking for full-time work but finds nothing except a single hour of employment during any given week, they are, according to the definition used for the U-3, considered "employed"—period. This one-hour employee is considered to be, for purposes of the U-3, in the same category as someone secure in a full-time job. Both meet the BLS threshold for being employed.

Similarly, someone who works full- or part-time for a salary that falls below the poverty line (which means, for a three-person household, they made around $20,000 per year in 2020 or $25,000 per year in 2024) is classified under the U-3 the same way as someone earning $1 million every month. In other words, under the prevailing measure of American unemployment, workers in wildly different circumstances—some quite comfortable and working full-time, others almost entirely marginalized and seeking full-time work with no luck—are viewed as one and the same. There's no statistical distinction for the purposes of the U-3.[7]

To be fair, the BLS simultaneously puts out somewhat more revealing data, known as the "U-6," which uses labor participation numbers. But this is not the lead number, and even the U-6 suffers from some of the same infirmities as the U-3 (namely, not considering wages).[8] And to emphasize, the BLS's U-3 is the very statistic fed to the public as the definitive unemployment figure—a number announced on the front page of the newspaper and on the radio, internet, and television screen twelve times a year.

When discussing these shortcomings with my colleagues at LISEP, we began considering whether we could remedy the attendant misperceptions by employing the same underlying data to provide analysts with an alternative statistic that was truer to lived experience. After weeks parsing the data and modeling the various nuances, we eventually came to the conclusion that a more accurate sense of the labor market could be unearthed only if we first distinguished between part-time workers who want full-time employment and full-time workers, and then distinguished between workers who are not surpassing a poverty wage and those who are. This would allow LISEP's studies to separate workers earning poverty wages, part-time workers seeking full-time employment, and the jobless into a new category of "the functionally unemployed."

In other words, gaining a true sense of the labor market requires that we either change whom the BLS considers employed and use our definition of functionally employed or, at the very least, put our functionally-employed numbers and the BLS-employed numbers side by side when the U-3 is published every month, explaining to the public the difference. Only then can we all gauge how workers are truly faring.

As it turns out, shifting the definitional frame as we suggest makes a huge difference in our understanding of employment reality—in Houston, among Hispanic women, and in this country generally.

First, consider Houston overall. Recall that the prevailing unemployment rate in the area, the U-3, was 4.9 percent in 2023—a remarkably low figure. But if you move both involuntary part-time workers (namely, those seeking full-time work) and poverty-wage workers into the unemployed category, the picture is starkly different. That resulting figure can fairly be labeled the *True* Rate of Unemployment (TRU). A full 23.9 percent of Houston's population—nearly a quarter of the population—was *functionally* unemployed in 2023.[9]

Think of that: At a moment when the prevailing view around the country, and certainly in Washington, was that joblessness was so rare that employers looking to hire might be forced to raise wages, one in ' every four workers in metro Houston was either making a poverty wage or subsisting on part-time work when they preferred to work full-time.[10]

And 2023 wasn't some outlier. Since 2000, the gap between the *prevailing* unemployment figure (the U-3) in the Houston area and the *functional* unemployment figure (the TRU) has vacillated between a low of 19.0 points, meaning at least one in every six workers was misleadingly classified as employed in the U-3, to a whopping 25.2 points.[i] This means a quarter of workers in the area were misleadingly classified as securely employed. In short, a great deal of the region's workforce is either subsisting on part-time work while hoping to find a full-time position or struggling in a full-time or part-time position that pays them a poverty wage. Yet that reality is shrouded by the U-3.

It's extremely troubling, too, that the two numbers paint very different pictures of the circumstances facing Houston's Hispanic female population. In 2023, the U-3 suggested 5.0 percent of Houston's Hispanic women were unemployed—a seemingly small slice of the overall population in Houston of Hispanic women. But at the same time, our functionally unemployed number, the TRU, for Houston's Hispanic women was a full 34.2 percent—a much bigger slice and a very sad reality indeed.

---

i The lowest gap corresponds to 2023, when the TRU was 23.9 percent and the U-3 was
   4.9 percent. The highest gap corresponds to 2005, when the TRU was 30.7 percent and the U-3
   was 5.5 percent.

In other words, even at this purportedly halcyon moment, one in three Hispanic Houstonian women were functionally unemployed. And that trend was persistent: For Hispanic women in the Houston metro area, *functional* unemployment has averaged a full 38.8 points higher than the official U-3 rate has reported over the past two decades or so.[ii] In 2009, a particularly egregious example, a mere 7.1 percent of Hispanic women were considered unemployed by the prevailing metric—but in reality, more than half (55 percent) were looking for work, enduring poverty wages, or trying to sustain themselves in part-time jobs when they wanted more hours.

What lessons can we draw from these disparities?

First, and most important, a closer look at the figures suggests that even in the best times, things are not good for many of the people whom the prevailing indicator considers employed. Houston is just one example of what is a nationwide phenomenon. For every single American who is considered *officially* unemployed, five more are *functionally* unemployed. Worse, for every Hispanic woman who is *officially* unemployed, seven more are *functionally* unemployed.[11] And that really shatters any notion that Hispanic women are keeping pace economically, regardless of what the official statistics suggest. Indeed, because so many are either earning poverty wages or having to accept part-time work when they want more, they are at quite a substantial disadvantage.

Second, the immediate shock born from comparing these two indexes, both arising from the same data, brings to the fore a dark reality: Relying on the *prevailing* measure of unemployment, the leading headline, causes policymakers and the American people

---

ii This average corresponds to the unweighted average of the annual TRU and U-3 percentage point difference for Hispanic women in Houston between 2000 and 2023.

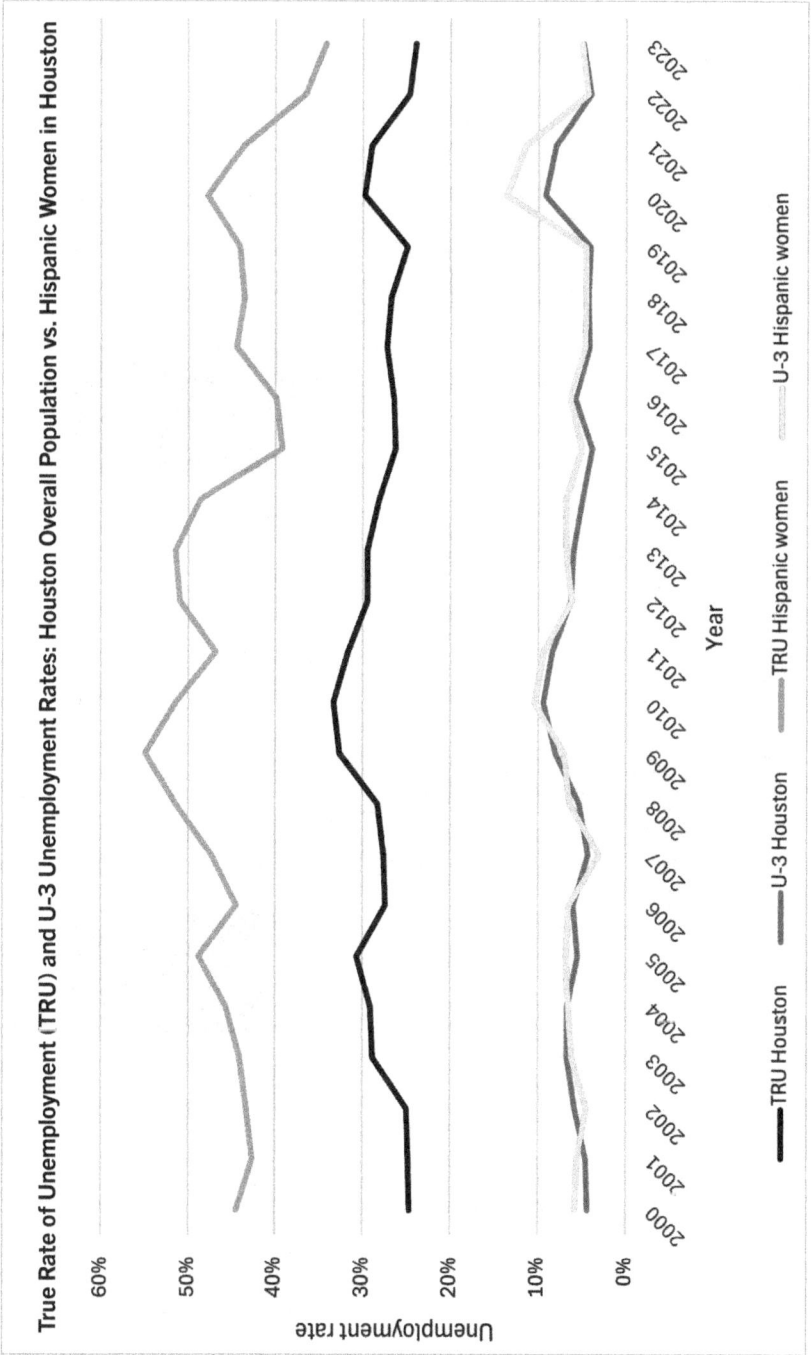

True Rate of Unemployment (TRU) and U-3 Unemployment Rates: Houston Overall Population vs. Hispanic Women in Houston

Legend: TRU Houston · U-3 Houston · TRU Hispanic women · U-3 Hispanic women

Y-axis: Unemployment rate (0%, 10%, 20%, 30%, 40%, 50%, 60%)

X-axis: Year (2000, 2001, 2002, 2003, 2004, 2005, 2006, 2007, 2008, 2009, 2010, 2011, 2012, 2013, 2014, 2015, 2016, 2017, 2018, 2019, 2020, 2021, 2022, 2023)

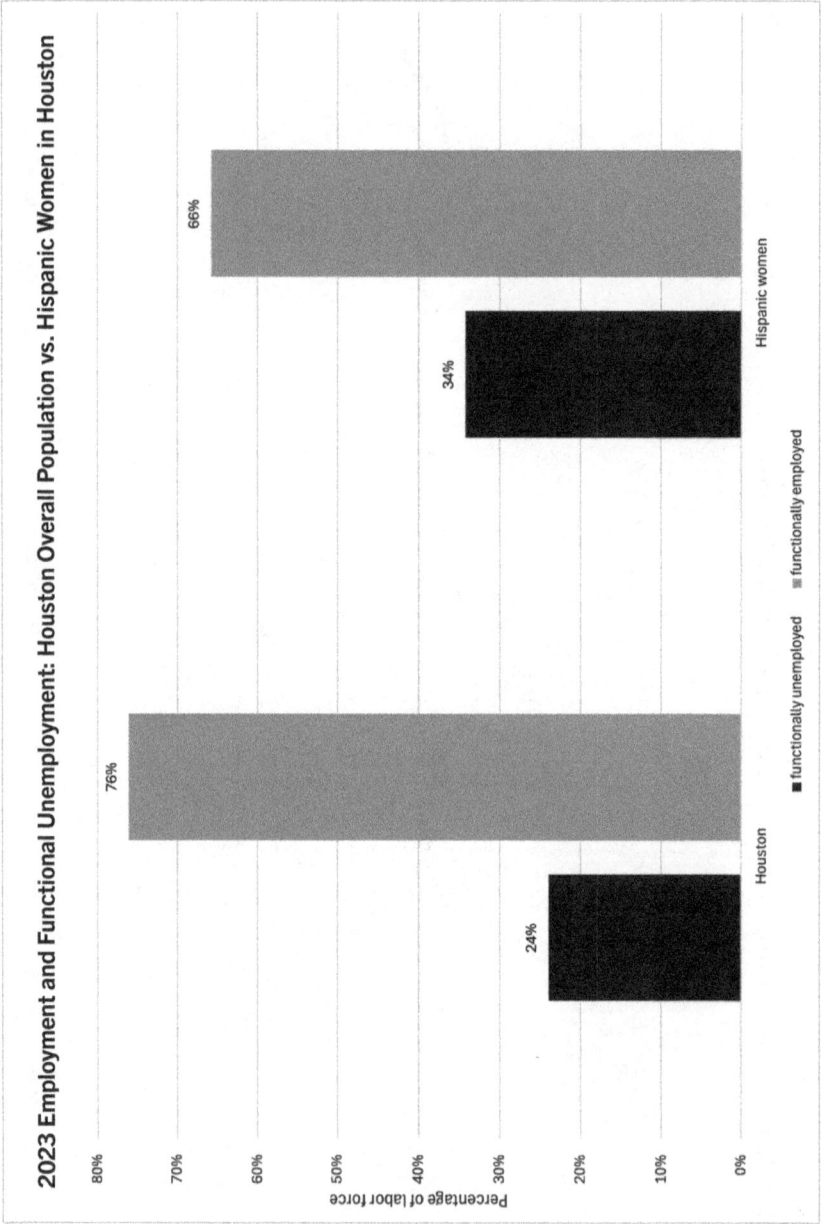

2023 Employment and Functional Unemployment: Houston Overall Population vs. Hispanic Women in Houston

generally to look at economic reality through a distorted and dangerous set of rose-colored glasses. These glasses give almost everyone a false sense of satisfaction, if not celebration, which obscures a much more accurate view of the economy. If only 4.9 percent of a region's population is unemployed, this suggests not only that the economy is humming along but that almost all who want a good job can find one that provides them with a modicum of comfort. However, in Houston as well as in the country as a whole, this is not the case.

In one sense, this should not be surprising. The reality we see with our eyes and hear with our ears, and that many face directly every day, is not rosy. Squalid tent communities are growing in many cities and there are rows of unpainted, and in some cases burnt-out, row houses in once-thriving places like Baltimore, St. Louis, Cleveland, and Detroit—places where the American Dream seemed plausible not long ago.[12] This story is true for the majority of Americans and, as if this were not bad enough, even worse in almost every case for women and minority communities.[13]

Returning for a moment to the plight of Hispanic women in Houston, the real numbers are depressing: Among those who are considered functionally unemployed, there is a ten-point gap between the general Houston population (23.9 percent) and the region's Hispanic women (34.2 percent). And for those looking to make a living, that distinction makes a world of difference.

But equally dispiriting is that the functional unemployment numbers for America overall are terrible. Even at a time when unemployment has been the lowest in fifty years—at 3.5 percent in 2023—the TRU was 23.3 percent, meaning that (as stated above) for every unemployed worker in the United States, an additional five were functionally unemployed.[14] In 2023, despite having a lower BLS unemployment rate than their male counterparts, American women continued to face a disproportionately higher rate of functional unemployment, at 28.3 percent—almost ten points higher than the 18.9 percent TRU for men. Black workers and Hispanic workers that year were also more likely to be functionally unemployed, with a TRU at 26 percent and 27.6 percent, respectively—significantly higher than the 21.9 percent rate for non-Hispanic White workers.

Finally, the fact that the current key headline statistic is so misleading is not just unsettling; it is enormously dangerous. Policymakers with their hands on the levers that drive our economy look at the headline statistics and see one reality, and yet, what everyday Americans experience—and what a more meaningful set of functional unemployment numbers reveal—is starkly different. Ignoring this reality gap will lead to spreading economic woes among a broader American public begging for different policy responses.

UNEMPLOYMENT–BUT THROUGH A GLASS DARKLY

Unemployment rates aren't just indicators—they themselves affect the economy. They shape how forecasters understand a region's broader trajectory, and they impact how the paragons of industry and commerce invest their resources, or don't.[15] To that end, the month-to-month figures can have such a profound effect on the market that the BLS maintains a strict protocol when releasing the figures. Only the president, the chair of the White House Council of Economic

Advisers, and a handful of senior US Treasury Department officials have access to the numbers before they are revealed to the public, and no executive branch official is permitted to comment on the data until at least an hour after its public release.[16] Although members of the press were once given a preview a half hour in advance, that privilege has more recently been withdrawn.[17]

But it's not just the economic impacts. Unemployment figures also shape popular, and certainly political, notions of where the economy is and where it's heading. And that's why the evidence from Houston, and indeed the national numbers cited above, are so troubling. Policymakers who make wide-ranging decisions about how to steer the economy—which programs should expand and which should contract, which regulations need updating and which can be left alone—often ground their judgments in their contemporary sense of the labor market. And if their impressions of the economy are shaped by wildly inflated notions of how many Americans enjoy full-time jobs providing middle-class compensation, they are likely making choices very different from those they would make if their impressions better reflected the reality on the ground.

Today's prevailing illusions weren't born of malevolence. Rather, the statistics simply haven't kept up with fundamental shifts in the labor market. Over the past several decades, the nation's labor market has changed, with an increasing proportion of workers involuntarily compelled to accept part-time work because of "business conditions."[18] And that, in a nutshell, is why the TRU provides a much more incisive view of what's actually happening in the workforce: It reflects the fact that someone who is *functionally* unemployed is in much the same circumstance as someone who is *actually* unemployed.

Whether you're earning a poverty wage, working a part-time job with little hope of finding something more, or sitting at home and looking for a job online, you're not in a very good place.

People with different political viewpoints can debate whether it's economically advantageous to have an economy replete with many part-time positions and low-wage jobs or, alternatively, a smaller universe of full-time positions that pay more. Perhaps, some will argue, it's more advantageous to have an increasingly fluid labor market so employees aren't "trapped" in jobs with long-term pensions. Others, of course, will strongly disagree.

What's less debatable is whether the labor market's evolution is changing the reality of what the labor market looks like today. As revealed by the statistics in Houston, it appears today as though very substantial portions of the labor force are employed in either "involuntary" part-time work or full-time work at poverty wages. Although comparable data from the postwar era is not available, we can conjecture that the U-3 and the TRU might have led economic analysts at that time to reach less divergent impressions, if only because a great proportion of jobs were full-time.[19] Today, however, the TRU is a full six times larger than the U-3, which means that in addition to every officially unemployed person there are five more functionally unemployed people. And that's the problem.

Nationally, in 2022, as some policymakers were celebrating record-low unemployment[20] and many in Washington were riven by worries that an overheated labor market would drive inflation,[21] the gap between the *prevailing* unemployment rate of 3.6 percent and the *functional* unemployment rate of 23.4 percent (low by historic standards, but high by nearly any other measure) was 19.8 percentage points.[22] In other words, nearly one of every five members of the labor force—over thirty-two million workers—was either making a poverty wage, working involuntarily in part-time jobs, or both.[23] Beyond that, six million people were entirely out of a job.[24] That's not a workforce tapped out of potential—it's one marked, at the bottom, by people who are desperately in need of good jobs. Yet most economic analyses at this time began with the notion that the labor market had rarely, if ever, been tighter.

It's not only the sheer size of the overall distortion created by the headline unemployment statistics that is highly troubling and dangerous. Also troubling is how the burden falls among disparate demographics. The burden of functional unemployment is not spread evenly across the American population. Across the workforce as a whole, the TRU is six times as high as the U-3 (as stated above), but among Hispanic women nationwide, the TRU is 34.1 percent—*eight* times higher than the U-3, which was 4.4 percent in 2023. And that's a thumbnail of how powerfully misleading the prevailing statistics have become: More than a quarter of the nation's female Hispanic workforce is considered "employed," even if workers are being forced to settle for part-time work, a poverty wage, or, regrettably, both.

On the whole, people miscast by the U-3 as employed are not lazily sitting at home. They aren't conniving to do the minimum necessary to qualify for some government-funded bounty. Rather, the Americans who are *officially* employed, but *functionally* unemployed, are either piecing together "a living" through part-time work or struggling to keep their heads above water in full-time jobs that pay a poverty wage. And this population is too heavily tilted toward minorities and women.

Consider one example: In 2018, Houston-area resident Violet Moya had taken a part-time job at a well-known national specialty store with the explicit expectation that if she worked hard, maintained a degree of scheduling flexibility, and served the company's customers well, she would eventually earn her way into a full-time position. Her bosses promised her nothing less. And for nearly two years, she was time and again given the impression that she was on the cusp of attaining the more regular schedule, additional hours, higher pay, and benefits that came with a full-time position. But that full-time position never materialized. Instead, when the Covid pandemic hit, Moya was laid off.[25]

And her story is typical. Huge swaths of America's working-age, "employed" population are toiling away in the hopes of landing a good job. But like Charlie Brown's football, it remains perpetually elusive.

Set aside any preconceived notions of what ails the American economy. The reality here is that a substantial portion of the positions now on offer to many Americans simply don't provide the sort of remuneration one expects to come with being employed. One-fifth of the nation's teachers, librarians, office clerks, and health care support workers work either part-time involuntarily or in positions that compensate them with less pay than what is required to lift them above the poverty line. And while, in some instances, that tracks with educational attainment—some workers who earn associate or bachelor's degrees might have better opportunities to climb the ladder and claim higher-paying jobs—in too many situations, workers who have already earned degrees do not reap the benefits and others have no such option to earn a better living.

Again, the point here is not that the data is inaccurate or even that the prevailing unemployment figure is purposefully misleading. It's simply that for economic analysts trying to make sense of broader conditions, financiers considering where to invest resources, or policymakers trying to shape an agenda that will serve the nation's broader prosperity, the U-3 is, at best, skirting the edge of a meaningful picture of reality. And that fact lies at the base of the problem: Lulled into thinking the labor market is fairly tight—and distracted from seeing the degree to which workers are desperate for better-compensated work—policymakers have allowed the nation's labor economy to evolve over the decades in a way that cuts against the broader public interest.

A SYSTEM OF PERVERSE INCENTIVES

When the U-3 was crafted as a new measure of unemployment in 1937, the nation's economic expectations were wildly different from those of today. Families were expected to boast a single breadwinner and a stay-at-home parent. In the decades that followed, blue-collar workers often were able to earn middle-class wages. Organized labor was more frequently able to extract from management the level of compensation that provided a modicum of prosperity.

But that scenario has changed over the years, for several reasons.

First, of course, social norms have evolved. During the Great Depression and for several decades thereafter, policymakers often worried about the implications of women streaming into the professional workforce when they had kids at home. What would become of the children? An early welfare program, Aid to Dependent Children (ADC, later renamed to Aid to Families with Dependent Children or AFDC) passed as part of 1935's Social Security Act, was designed so that single mothers lost welfare benefits if they gained employment, inducing them to serve exclusively as full-time parents.[26] Any deviation from the norms later illustrated in 1950s television shows like *The Honeymooners* and *Leave It to Beaver* was deemed a threat to the social fabric.

But the Great Depression and World War II made women's participation in the workforce a necessity.[27] After the end of the war, women who were displaced by men reentering the labor force found work in clerical roles, and the stigma—and in some cases outright bans—on married women's participation in the labor force began to slowly wane.[28] However, infrastructure for supportive childcare did not keep up. That then required many more working parents to find work schedules that would allow them to fulfill their professional responsibilities *and* to take care of their children—a demand that, in a society where school tends to release in the midafternoon, was not always easy. By 2022, a greater proportion of American workers were being compelled to take part-time work due to childcare concerns than at any other time in recent history. That number was then surpassed in 2023.[29]

Second, the American economy shifted overall from an industrial to a service-oriented base, which changed the cocktail of job opportunities. After bottoming out in 2010, manufacturing jobs have begun to return to the United States over the past several years.[30] But that return follows decades of decline in industrial jobs, a shift born in part from offshoring and in larger part by gains in productivity—all while technology has made it possible for plants and factories to produce more and better products with less labor.[31] America's manufacturing sector produces twice as much as it did in 1979, but employment in the sector has fallen from a fifth to less than a tenth of the workforce.[32] And as much as that might have been a boon for the financial markets, it took a toll on the industrial workforce.

The result has shifted the sorts of jobs that prevail within the American economy. The positions that have come online in the years since the manufacturing-job collapse have, to a disproportionate degree, been focused on work that cannot so easily be replaced by technology or overseas workers. Many of these are service-sector jobs.[33] For a variety of reasons, most of which are beyond the scope of this analysis, a narrower slice of the service-sector workforce has been organized into unions that bargain collectively. More than a fifth of the private-sector workforce was unionized in 1979, but that figure had fallen to a mere 6 percent in 2023.[34] And the result of this broad-based shift is that a growing share of workers are seeking jobs in sectors of the economy that were not represented to nearly the same degree when the U-3 was developed as a primary economic indicator.[35]

What are these jobs?[36] In 2023, more than 9.9 million American jobs were in retail or similar transaction-focused occupations[iii]—the people working behind the counter at a store in the mall or as telemarketers or door-to-door salespeople. Five and a half million jobs were in

---

iii To give a more granular picture, LISEP selected occupations from the "employed persons by detailed occupation and age" table of the BLS's labor force statistics from the Current Population Survey and reported the total number of workers who were sixteen years old and older. Retail and similar occupations were identified as first-line supervisors of retail-sales workers; cashiers; counter and rental clerks; parts salespeople; retail salespeople; sales representatives; wholesale and manufacturing workers; telemarketers; door-to-door sales workers; news and street vendors; and related workers.

groundskeeping and janitorial work.[iv] Many jobs, nearly 4.2 million in 2023, were personal care and service occupations, a category that includes both childcare workers and hairdressers.[v] These employment categories existed in the 1950s, of course. Employers have long needed people to sell clothing in stores, check guests into hotels, and clean offices overnight. But these employees now represent a larger proportion of the overall workforce.[37] This is not necessarily a bad thing, as long as work conditions and pay are adequate and enable workers to provide for themselves and, if applicable, their families. Too often, college-educated individuals unintentionally—or intentionally—undervalue manual labor and domestic work. This book challenges this notion, focusing on whether full-time work, regardless of its nature, offers a living wage for those seeking it.

Finally, the job market has evolved because employers have embraced a new mentality. In the aftermath of World War II, prevailing managerial wisdom throughout many of the nation's heavy industrial sectors and elsewhere was that it was financially advantageous to retain employees through long stretches of their careers. To avoid enduring the costs brought about by high turnover and strikes,

---

iv Groundskeeping and janitorial jobs include first-line supervisors of housekeeping and janitorial workers; first-line supervisors of landscaping, lawn service, and groundskeeping workers; janitors and building cleaners; maids and housekeeping cleaners; pest control workers; landscaping and groundskeeping workers; tree trimmers and pruners; and other grounds maintenance workers.

v Personal care and service occupations include supervisors of personal care and service workers; animal trainers and caretakers; gambling services workers; ushers, lobby attendants, and ticket takers; other entertainment attendants and related workers; embalmers, crematory operators, and funeral attendants; morticians, undertakers, and funeral arrangers; barbers; hairdressers, hairstylists, and cosmetologists; manicurists and pedicurists; skincare specialists; other personal appearance workers; baggage porters, bellhops, and concierges; tour and travel guides; childcare workers; exercise trainers and group fitness instructors; recreation workers; residential advisors; and all other personal care and service workers.

it appeared better to incentivize employees to continue working within that same realm season upon season, year upon year. Workers were induced to stay, in many cases, through "defined benefit" pensions—an annuity they earned through years of service to a single firm.[38] Moreover, after the United Auto Workers' "Treaty of Detroit" was enacted, industrial unions generally acquiesced to a system where health care and other benefits were provisioned through employers rather than through the government or a private marketplace.[39] These are the sorts of steady jobs that the U-3 might have been able to measure quantitatively.

But as the contours of the broader economy and labor market shifted through subsequent decades, employers—particularly those in service-oriented industries—have seen more benefit in adopting (or are economically required to adopt) the opposite approach. It seems better now to have a larger pool of part-time workers than a shorter roster of full-time employees. That way, companies can expeditiously grow or shrink the size of their workforce in real time to meet demand.[40] If, for example, it behooves a business to stay open late on weekend nights during certain months of the year, the company can add hours for a specific pool of workers, only some of whom may be available during those times.

This broader shift offers employers a host of ancillary advantages as well, many of which serve as perverse incentives to disenfranchise US workers. Businesses that do not want to pay the overtime wages mandated for full-time employees can sidestep that expense by churning shifts of part-time help, with each employee contributing fewer hours and avoiding the overtime threshold. Beyond that, part-time workers rarely receive the benefits full-time workers are guaranteed; in early 2024, only 26 percent of part-time workers in the private sector had access to medical benefits, compared with 87 percent of full-time workers.[41] Businesses are not required to offer health insurance to employees who work fewer than thirty hours.[42] In short, the advantages of incentivizing employees to remain in a company's employ on a full-time basis for years now often pale in comparison to the upside of maintaining a longer roster of part-time workers. And employers have adjusted accordingly.

Unfortunately for large swaths of America's workforce, this massive change in the contours of the labor market has been almost entirely obscured by the U-3. According to this decades-old measure, two unemployed workers—one who secures a unionized, forty-hour-per-week, forty-dollar-per-hour job with health insurance and benefits, and another who is compelled (due to lack of alternative opportunities) to accept a part-time, twelve-dollar-per-hour job at a local retailer—meet the same statistical threshold: They *both* qualify as being employed. They are tallied in the same category. So if someone on the outside wants to understand the state of the labor market, they are left blind to this glaring reality: Among those traditionally counted as employed are workers subject to wildly different economic trajectories.

THE BEST DISINFECTANT

It is, of course, impossible to know exactly how a better understanding of economic realities might affect the decisions of those in power—particularly when it comes to politics and policymaking. Some elected officials may be so ensconced in their ideological convictions that drastically different statistics from the accepted norm would have little, if any, impact on their policy inclinations. Some elected officials with real power in Washington clearly believe, with almost a religious fervor, that government is invariably either the cause of—or, alternatively, the salve for—every economic challenge we face. They presume, respectively, that if there were just more government spending or significantly less public largesse, things would get better.

"It's a recognition that Democrats want more government intervention than ever," according to one analysis; said another, "Others, of course, . . . would make it harder for the government to enact any regulations at all."[43] But for most, even those who claim to be entirely of one extreme or the other, different circumstances do require different solutions. And that's the rub: If, in fact, the government responds differently when faced with divergent economic circumstances, then perception can change policy, potentially in drastic ways.

Fortunately, *most* elected officials are humble enough to set aside at least some of their prior conceptions in the face of certain economic circumstances. During the Covid-19 pandemic, for example, even members of Congress who were most skeptical of government interventions were inclined to support new government spending.[44] And in the early 1990s, even members who believed the public sector could productively play a *larger* role in the economy were convinced there was an economic benefit to lowering private borrowing costs by balancing the federal budget.[45] If an ideological predisposition doesn't fit neatly with the circumstances on the ground, savvy politicians know it behooves them to adjust their approach. This is why it's entirely plausible that a more precise set of economic suppositions might prompt an economic debate, if not an economic agenda, that is substantially and substantively different from what prevails today.

Take, as an example, the circumstances that confronted policy-makers in early 2018. The economy was humming along at 3 percent annual growth.[46] In less than a decade, the S&P index had nearly tripled in value since its previous trough in 2009.[47] And according to the U-3, unemployment had fallen to a near-record low of 4 per-cent.[48] Someone who took that last figure at face value might well have assumed that there was no need for a policy to boost the labor market—that nearly everyone eager for work was able to find it. The question before the president and Congress at the time was how to shape national economic policy in response to these numbers. Perhaps quite reasonably given the economic indicators, the White House pro-posed cutting federal funding for state and local job training programs by a third. One such measure was a proposed 23 percent cut in the Job Corps program, which provides education and training to young people at 121 sites around the country.[49]

The question, today, is whether these policies would have seemed reasonable, even to those who are most skeptical of job training pro-grams, if the prevailing belief wasn't that unemployment had fallen to 4.1 percent (as the U-3 suggested), but rather that nearly a quarter of the nation's workforce—27.4 percent of the labor market—was func-tionally unemployed.[vi] In the end, the cuts were largely canceled when partisan opposition on Capitol Hill emerged to reject the president's budget.[50] But the question remains: Would anyone have even even *con-sidered* these sorts of cuts if the general understanding had been that more than a quarter of the workforce was forced to survive without a full-time, living-wage job?

---

vi As of January 2018.

Take another example: In 2021, the Veteran Rapid Retraining Assistance Program (VRRAP) was passed as a part of the American Rescue Plan. It allocated money to the US Department of Veterans Affairs to retrain eligible veterans, giving them the skills needed to work in well-paid, in-demand professions. Under the bill, eligible veterans are defined as individuals who, among other requirements, were unemployed due to the Covid pandemic. But at the time of the bill's passage, more than 225,000 *fewer* veterans were *functionally* employed compared with the precrisis period. In March 2021, while the U-3 for veterans was 5.3 percent, the TRU for veterans was 19.4 percent.

All of this is to say: *The framing of the issue matters.* The statistical indicators that prevail in public discourse profoundly shape the public's understanding of the economy, and the prevailing view of what's happening in the economy determines public policy. From a policymaking perspective, a world where a tiny fraction of the population is unemployed is wildly different from one where a fifth, or even a quarter, of workers are subsisting without a full-time, living-wage job. When the information becomes more accurate, the range of reasonable policymaking options changes.

This may seem obvious in questions of war and peace: Washington would be much less likely to launch a military attack on a country that had no belligerent intentions against the United States, but in the event of an attack by that country, the policy options would change dramatically. The same is true for the economy: Circumstances matter. Perceptions matter. Public policy is a function of how those who work along the corridors of power, and their constituents, understand the world around them.

Americans today, both in the general population and among elite policymakers, are seeing the nation's labor market through a glass darkly. Their perspective, based on imperfect statistics, is askew. The U-3, which drastically undercounts the prevalence of *functional* unemployment in the country, might well have been a good measure of joblessness when it was crafted nearly a century ago. But today it serves primarily to mask a much grimmer reality. As the TRU reveals, significantly more of America's working population is struggling than prevailing figures would indicate. Policymakers are making decisions based on an entirely distorted view of the middle and lower end of the labor market. And the impact, as the next chapters discuss, can be profound.

Chapter 2

True Weekly Earnings

IN SEARCH OF A GOOD JOB

For all that Americans may rue the scourge of inequality, few question whether certain professions are rightfully compensated more than others. Those compelled to spend years earning advanced degrees—doctors, for example—generally earn more per hour than those whose professions require fewer years of formal education. And by the prevailing standard, that seems fair enough. Most Americans have long celebrated "pull yourself up by your bootstraps" stories—exalting the house painter or farmhand or chauffeur who works for years so that the next generation is able to graduate with a college degree, earn a more generous living, and propel the third generation even further. That trajectory is an indelible element of the American Dream.

But even among professions that don't require college diplomas or advanced degrees, certain jobs are deemed more worthy of additional compensation. Jobs that are unusually dangerous, for example, or those demanding longer hours, more arduous labor, or a higher degree of inconvenience, seem deserving of higher pay. To that end, construction work is some of the most desirable among the blue-collar professions. Those who do the gritty, demanding labor of erecting new buildings are often better compensated on an hourly basis than those who are engaged in other sorts of blue-collar work.[1] And that, in common parlance, makes it a better job.

Of course, wage *rates* aren't a perfect stand-in for job *quality*. And that's not just because some professions are more dangerous, demanding, or inconvenient. It's because not all positions provide the same number of hours, the same continuity of schedule, or the same benefits. Bank tellers don't earn particularly extravagant salaries, for example, but those working at a local bank branch often presume their work will remain constant in terms of location and hours, all twelve months of the year. Moreover, as the BLS reports, banks offer avenues for advancement, such as to a position as a loan officer or in sales—sometimes without an additional degree.[2]

That's not true for everyone working in construction. Roofers, for example, can't work during the winter months in many parts of the United States—nor can many presume that they'll be moved up into management if they stick with the same company for years, particularly without additional business training.[3] So, when assessing job quality for construction workers, it's important to weigh the high hourly rate against the reality that there will be days and weeks when they're bound to earn nothing at all.

The underlying issue here centers not just on the nature of construction work (as it compares with other professions), or even on the nuanced differences between those jobs that provide a steady income and those that have periods of what economists call "slack"—that is, times when the supply of labor exceeds employers' needs.[4] The core question is how Americans generally understand what is, and what is not, a "good" job. What does someone need to earn in order to feel they have a shot at the American Dream?

The previous chapter looked squarely at the *percentage* of employed people in the United States and, as we determined, the prevailing statistic known as "unemployment" does everyone a disservice by shrouding those who are *functionally* unemployed. Having a job does not necessarily mean that you have a *good* job, let alone that you have the ability to pursue the American Dream. To glean a clearer picture, you really have to take into consideration what a job's compensation allows an earner to afford. This chapter and the next one focus on quality of life. Here, we'll address how much workers actually earn; in the next chapter, we'll concentrate on what those earnings enable them to purchase.

Here, again, the federal Bureau of Labor Statistics sets the standard when it comes to collecting the economic data, publishing the Current Population Survey from microdata collected by the US Census Bureau. For decades, the agency has tracked what workers are paid in various locations doing various jobs.[5] And in order to make it possible for analysts to compare earnings from one type of work to the next, or from one moment in time to another, the BLS reports quarterly on the usual weekly earnings, known widely as "median wages."[6] The underlying intuition is simple and straightforward: If you lined up all the full-time employees who worked for at least thirty-five hours during the previous week in order of their weekly earnings, the person directly in the middle earns the median wage.

At first glance, this appears to be an intuitive way of comparing wages. For that reason, policymakers, financial analysts on Wall Street, and stakeholders across the economy have long used median wages to gauge the *quality* of the job market: If median wages are rising, it would seem reasonable to presume that people are earning more. If they're down, the opposite may be presumed. But as we'll see, for a whole variety of reasons, the BLS's median-wage statistic distorts reality.[7]

THE UNSEEN UNEMPLOYED

If wages are the most salient measure of job quality, you might presume that weekly medians would rise when the economy is humming and that they would tumble during hard times. But something odd happened during recent bouts of economic turmoil: As the economy went into near freefall during the early months of the Covid-19 pandemic, the percentage of Americans who were functionally unemployed (as delineated in the previous chapter) rose from 25.7 percent in the first quarter of 2020 to 32.9 percent in the second quarter. But at the same time, BLS-reported median earnings rose 7 percent.[8]

For those paying close attention, something appeared to be awry. Were the people raising alarms eliciting unwarranted concern? The explanation, as we'll see, centered largely on the fact that the prevailing median-wage statistic was, and remains, methodologically unsound. Counterintuitively, it rises during downtimes because Americans with lower-paying jobs are laid off.

The prevailing BLS statistic only considers the wages of full-time employees who are *presently* employed. So, the moment a low-wage factory worker receives a pink slip, her salary is deleted from the sample altogether. In short, the prevailing wage indicator doesn't measure wages across the whole of the labor force—it measures only wages for employees who are employed full-time at a specific moment. The unemployed and the underemployed are *statistically* disappeared.[9]

That, then, explains the statistical anomaly: In downtimes, employers tightening their belts often lay off, in whole or in part, low-wage employees—the salespeople manning the registers, the cleaners sweeping the factory floor, the men and women moving equipment in the warehouse. And when those lower-wage employees are laid off, a company's median salary often rises because higher-wage employees claim the midpoint. When this happens across the whole economy, median wages tick up for the same reason.[10]

This strange statistical blip may be best illustrated by the plight of "temporary workers"—namely, the workers hired (usually on a full-time basis) to fill in for a short time only or take jobs that are unlikely to last over the long term. When a company needs help only temporarily—to move inventory during a busy season or to work the sales floor during the holidays—they often add temporary workers on their full-time payroll. Because these workers tend to earn more meager wages than permanently hired full-time employees, hiring them brings median wages down.[11]

The story, of course, doesn't end there. When the busy season ends, those salaries are deleted from the payrolls. This is particularly pointed during downtimes: While a "mere" 5.3 percent of the nation's nonfarm jobs disappeared between December 2007 and June 2009, during the Great Recession, almost a third of the nation's *temporary* jobs were eliminated.[12] Jobs that were better compensated remained.

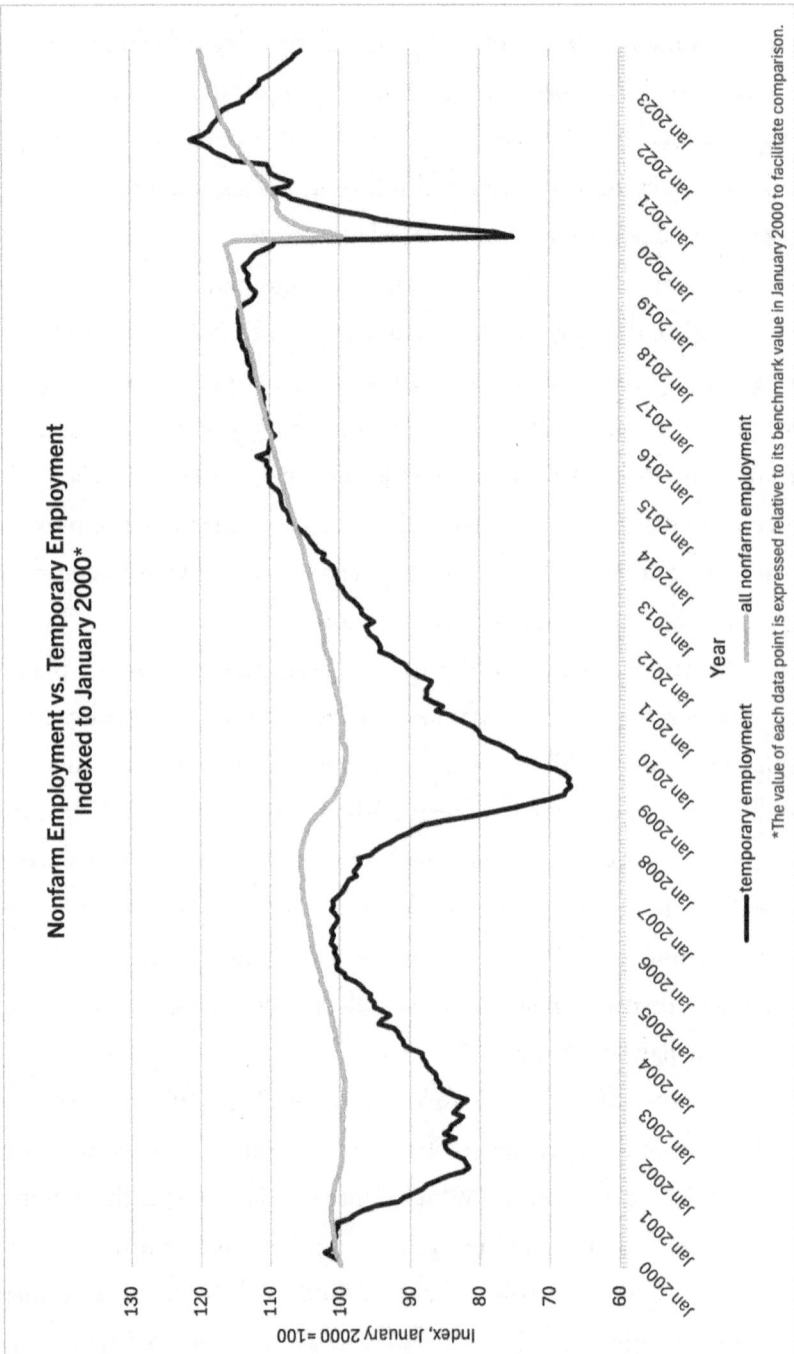

Nonfarm Employment vs. Temporary Employment
Indexed to January 2000*

Index, January 2000 = 100

Year

temporary employment   all nonfarm employment

*The value of each data point is expressed relative to its benchmark value in January 2000 to facilitate comparison.

And the perverse impact was that the median-wage indicator rose because the zero dollars that laid-off workers were now earning was not factored into the statistical methodology.[13]

THE ELUSIVE SECOND SHIFT

It would be one thing if the headline median-wage indicator simply overlooked the unemployed. The statistics could then be corrected simply by adding the jobless back into the sample used to calculate wages. But the headline median-wage indicator also excludes another crucial slice of the labor force from the sample—namely, those who work part-time.

If, for example, a part-time employee's hours are cut during a recession such that they take home less pay, their diminished income has no bearing whatsoever on the median-wage indicator. And of course, that sort of shift is widely prevalent during moments of economic turmoil.[14] But not only then.

In the previous chapter, we noted that part-time workers count as employed even if they can only find a few hours of part-time work each week. In the median-wage indicator, however, those workers are ignored altogether—the part-time wages are not factored in. And, of course, that's a substantial portion of employment—sometimes as much as a fifth,[15] most of whom subsist at the low end of the wage spectrum.[16] In the food service industry, for example, about 60 percent of waiters and waitresses, and about 75 percent of hosts and hostesses, work part-time; however, the median wage for these occupations is determined exclusively by the wages drawn by the remaining employees working on a full-time basis. Half of all dental hygienists work part-time, but the median wage for dental hygienists is determined exclusively by the other half working full-time.[17]

The percentage of workers accepting part-time work due to poor business conditions—that is, employees with no choice but to accept when their employer chooses to slash their hours—has increased since the 1960s.[18] And part-time workers make, on average, 30 percent less per hour than their full-time counterparts.[19] Yet because earnings are gauged exclusively on the basis of full-time workers, the prevailing wage statistic does not take this portion of the labor force into account whatsoever. And that pushes the median-wage indicator well above the true median wage.

Now, set aside the fact that the prevailing indicator gives this false impression—that the median wages for *all* workers in a certain category are defined by the median wages for only *full-time* workers—and consider another flaw in the conventional system: What happens when an employer decides to replace full-time workers with part-time workers making a reduced salary? In many cases, those part-time employees are offered fewer, if any, benefits and no health insurance. But this change in median wages is *also* lost to the indicator. So, a department store that replaces many of its full-time workers making twenty dollars per hour with part-time workers making fifteen dollars per hour is paying, in the aggregate, less per hour. But the median-wage indicator wouldn't pick up that change and might even rise if the remaining full-time workforce enjoyed higher salaries.

As discussed in the previous chapter, many companies now employ strategies designed to cull their full-time workers in favor of part-time employees who can be deployed more flexibly at a lower cost. Huge swaths of the American workforce have been negatively impacted by the change, but this well-reported upheaval in the labor market isn't being reflected in the headline statistics. And so those using BLS indicators to understand the economy often unwittingly fail to account for this profound shift.

SOLVING THE PROBLEM OF SLACK

These two core oversights in the prevailing indicator—failing to account for both the unemployed and those engaged in part-time work—have a particularly perverse effect on those engaged in professions that are subject to what economists term "seasonal slack."

An employee's weekly earnings are in practice assumed to be constant over the entire quarter, even if they earn those wages only periodically. In other words, what they make one week will continue indefinitely on a weekly basis. Meanwhile, the *annual* income of a person who works all twelve months of the year will be different from that of someone who works only nine months, even if their weekly wages are the same during the nine months when both are on the job.[i] The headline median-wage metric fails to account for this wrinkle, however, and the ensuing distortion is profound.

Consider again the case of construction workers, 80 percent of whom are considered full-time when they're working, and many of whom earn relatively robust wages during those periods of employment.[20] It's a distortion to compare what a construction

---

i To annualize income, logic would suggest adding up the weekly earnings across all four quarters (fifty-two weeks), but this leads to inaccurate conclusions if the worker does not work the entirety of all four quarters. That caveat is not expressed in the reporting of the usual weekly earnings (median wages).

worker makes on a weekly basis for, say, forty weeks of the year (that is, when the weather allows) with the smaller salary a bank teller makes for all fifty-two weeks. During the summer months, the *weekly* wage of the construction worker may outpace the bank teller's, but the bank teller makes more over the course of a full year. Yet the weekly wage statistic would give the impression that the construction worker is engaged in more remunerative work.

Taken together, the median-wage indicator's shortcomings are clear: Unemployed workers and part-time workers are essentially invisible, and seasonal workers subject to periods of slack are only counted when they're working. As a result, wages in America are refracted through a lens that materially overstates what American workers are earning.

Set aside how many Americans are functionally employed, as discussed in the previous chapter. Set aside, as well, how much it may take to maintain any certain lifestyle, as will be discussed in subsequent chapters. The upshot is that analysts and policymakers today make decisions based on incorrect impressions of America's earnings. Fortunately, we need not rely on the prevailing measure.

The Bureau of Labor Statistics compiles data for the entire population, with the labor force as a subset. And the data focuses on *everyone* in the labor force—not just those with full-time jobs. By adding back into the sample workers who are unemployed but seeking employment, and workers who are employed in part-time positions, we can fairly readily craft a more comprehensive, accurate indicator of *true* median wages. That's precisely what LISEP has done, creating what we have labeled True Weekly Earnings (TWE) to gauge the true quality of the nation's job market.

A MORE ACCURATE RENDERING

As we'll see, a look back at earnings through the lens provided by the TWE—rather than that of usual weekly earnings, the prevailing indicator—paints a very different picture of economic reality through the decades. Most important, median earnings generally overstate True Weekly Earnings by about one-fifth.[21]

As of the first quarter of 2024, for example, workers at the median were earning a full $9,778 less per year than what the prevailing indicator reported. Importantly, the TWE also reveals how the median-wage indicator undermines broader efforts to understand the economy. Wages *should* serve as a canary in the coal mine of recession-oriented statistics, by falling *before* moments of turmoil and recovering only after the economy is back on track. But as discussed above, that's not what the prevailing indicator suggests.

Take, as an example, the Great Recession, when the bottom fell out of the economy between the last quarter of 2007 and the second quarter of 2009. Much like what would later happen during the Covid pandemic, prevailing median-wage statistics *rose* by 3.9 percent—an indication that seemed to suggest the economy was being buoyed even as the mortgage bubble burst.[22] Those who understood the true state of the economy were dubious: Why would wages rise when businesses were shedding employees? Indeed, it was during this period that the TRU grew from 27.9 percent to 33.3 percent.

This anomaly would have been resolved if the workers excluded from the prevailing indicator had been woven back into the statistic. People were being laid off. Full-time employees were being forced into part-time jobs. Those in part-time positions were having their hours slashed. Combined, those changes were devastating the economy.

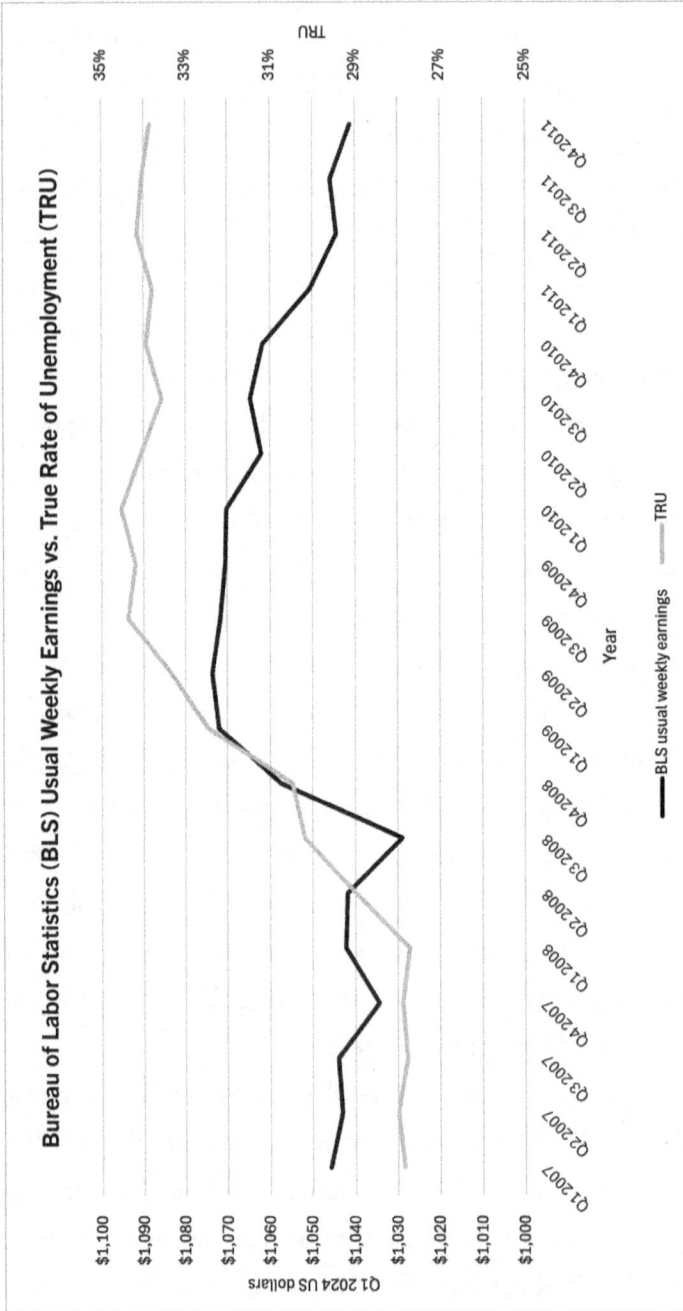

Bureau of Labor Statistics (BLS) Usual Weekly Earnings vs. True Rate of Unemployment (TRU)

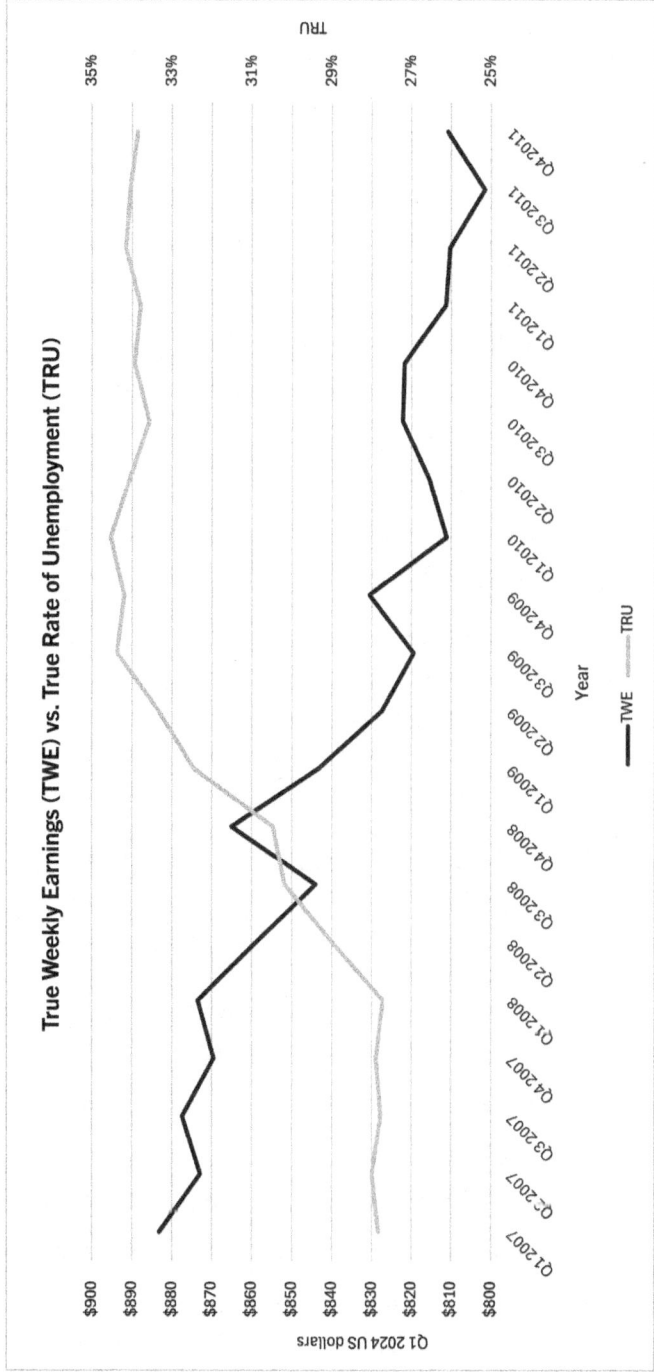

True Weekly Earnings (TWE) vs. True Rate of Unemployment (TRU)

TRU

35%

33%

31%

29%

27%

25%

Q1 2024 US dollars

$900

$890

$880

$870

$860

$850

$840

$830

$820

$810

$800

Year

Q1 2007
Q2 2007
Q3 2007
Q4 2007
Q1 2008
Q2 2008
Q3 2008
Q4 2008
Q1 2009
Q2 2009
Q3 2009
Q4 2009
Q1 2010
Q2 2010
Q3 2010
Q4 2010
Q1 2011
Q2 2011
Q3 2011
Q4 2011

TWE ——— TRU

And that underlying reality, hidden by the prevailing indicator, was made plain by the TWE, which more appropriately *fell* during the same period by 4.8 percent.

The same phenomenon repeated itself in even greater contrast in certain sectoral analyses. Recall that the Great Recession originated primarily from an exploded mortgage bubble, and the demand for new housing fell off considerably.[23] The impacts rippled out. Between 2006 and 2010, for example, output within the construction sector fell by almost 30 percent.[24] The lack of demand compelled many construction firms to either lay off their employees or put them on a "wait list." Given those circumstances, many would have expected wages in the construction sector to plummet. But the prevailing statistics suggested the housing market collapse had a *positive* impact on real wages (meaning wages accounting for the effects of inflation). From 2006 (the peak of the bubble) to 2010 (widely regarded as the trough for the subprime crisis[25]), real wages as measured by the median wages actually rose 2.8 percent.

That was a statistical illusion: As the TWE reveals, inflation-adjusted wages in construction fell by 6.2 percent, meaning that workers were, according to the median, feeling the full effect of the recession. This purely sectoral evidence of the TWE's heightened accuracy suggests that in addition to being remarkably more reliable in measuring wages, the TWE is also much better at describing the broader shape of the economy.

As highlighted in the previous chapter, Washington politicians, analysts, and economists are poorly served by the inaccurate picture they are forced to accept of who is, and who is not, employed. The same phenomenon plagues our public understanding of earnings:

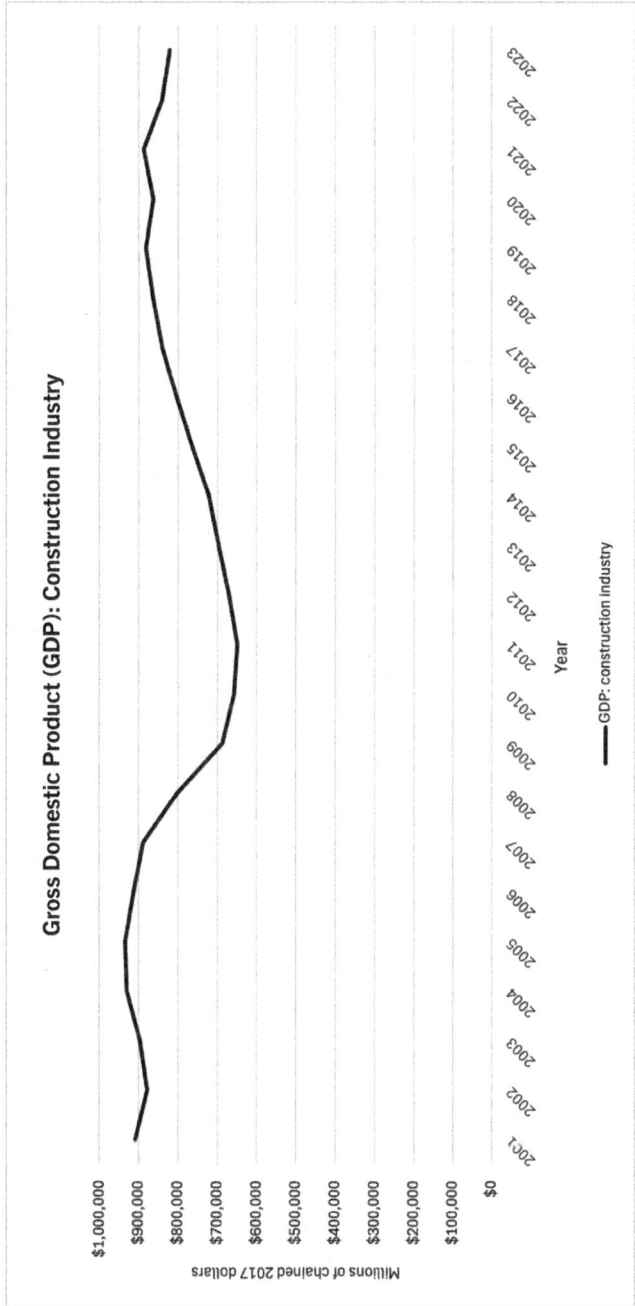

Gross Domestic Product (GDP): Construction Industry

Millions of chained 2017 dollars

$1,000,000
$900,000
$800,000
$700,000
$600,000
$500,000
$400,000
$300,000
$200,000
$100,000
$0

2001 2002 2003 2004 2005 2006 2007 2008 2009 2010 2011 2012 2013 2014 2015 2016 2017 2018 2019 2020 2021 2022 2023

Year

— GDP: construction industry

Prevailing statistics have given both policymakers and the public at large a fanciful notion of important developments in the labor market. And that has had, and continues to have, profound implications for those trying to steer the economy toward growth and shared prosperity. What's worse is that these distortions sharpen during recessions, which is when accurate economic indicators are needed most to successfully drive economic policy.

A CLEARER PICTURE

Here's the reality: The TWE demonstrates that in the first quarter of 2024, the median worker took home 17 percent *less* than the prevailing statistic indicates—which is $9,700 less than we are led to believe, assuming a fifty-two-week work year.[ii] And that disparity has held for years, in good and bad times alike: The TWE medians have come in between just 76 percent and 86 percent of the prevailing figure in every quarter since 2000. The gap narrows in times of expansion (as more unemployed and part-time workers find full-time positions) and peaks in times of recession (when full-time workers lose their jobs or are shunted into part-time positions outside the prevailing indicator's gaze).

Before we delve into the policy implications more directly, take a moment to consider how that divergence plays out in the public mind. Americans today who are making the TWE median wage are likely under the misimpression, if they look at prevailing median-earning

---

ii The figure is actually starker, at $9,830 (in Q1, 2024 dollars), when applying annualized differences without rounding decimals beforehand.

statistics, that they are in fact earning materially less than the median earner. Setting aside the economic implications, the purely emotional takeaway of thinking you are in the bottom half of earners when you're actually at (or even *above*) the median is potentially profound. People working hard and playing by the rules are likely to come away from their toil believing that they're unable to earn what others in similar places are earning. The prevailing wage is fodder for popular resentment, which itself has the potential to stimulate a host of social, political, and economic woes.

But the impacts aren't just on the nation's psyche—the effects on policymakers may be even more direct. Many experts and analysts are aware of the prevailing statistic's shortcomings, so they discount its importance. If policymakers want more accurate data, they are compelled to look to a separate US Census Bureau survey called the Current Population Survey Annual Social and Economic Supplement.[26] But the Census Bureau's data is delayed by nine months, meaning that it's almost useless to those making policy in real time.

Happily, however, the TWE (computed with the monthly Current Population Survey) largely correlates with the Census Bureau's figures, yielding a correlation coefficient of 0.95.[27] Accordingly, the TWE could offer policymakers the best of both worlds: the accuracy of the Census Bureau figures and the alacrity of the BLS metric. Had the TWE been available in 2008, for example—when the prevailing wage indicator was still signaling that wages were on the rise—few would have been fooled into believing that the economy was in anything but a crisis.

Finally, the TWE provides a much more accurate measure of the nation's *racial* wage gap. To look back at the prevailing indicator through the years, you might conclude that White and Black wages rise and fall in tandem. But the TWE reveals that Black and White workers are not, by any means, traveling the same path. Black workers, who disproportionately earn nearer the bottom of the pay scale, are hit harder during recessions and suffer the impacts for longer.[28] And the aggregate impact is really quite dramatic: The median Black worker earned 21 percent less than the median White worker in the first quarter of 2024, according to the headline BLS statistic; the TWE measured the difference more accurately at a 27 percent deficit.[iii] And the racial wage gap has actually grown. The 27 percent deficit in 2024 is up from a 25 percent deficit in 1982 and a 23 percent deficit in 2000.[iv] We're headed in the wrong direction.

The gender gap is similarly glaring. The prevailing median-wage indicator suggests that women earned eighty-three cents on the male-earned dollar during the first quarter of 2024. But the TWE, taking a fuller measure of the American labor force, revealed that women—who disproportionately accept part-time positions—actually earned only seventy-nine cents on the dollar as compared to men.

We cannot know with complete confidence how public perceptions and policy choices would change if the TWE replaced today's headline indicator. Perhaps, if they had had wage data anchored in reality, the Obama White House and the Federal Reserve would

---

iii The deficit between Hispanic workers and non-Hispanic White workers was 29 percent in the first quarter of 2024, according to the BLS's median wages. The TWE suggests the same at 29 percent, even as the median earnings for both Hispanic workers and non-Hispanic White workers was lower than the metrics reported by the BLS.

iv Because this earnings data is not adjusted for seasonal fluctuations, the deficits between Black and White earnings refer to the first quarters of 1982 and 2000 in this comparison. Specifically, the Black-White earnings gap was 24.7 percent in the first quarter of 1982, 23.1 percent in the first quarter of 2000, and 27.2 percent in the first quarter of 2024.

Black True Weekly Earnings (TWE) / White True Weekly Earnings Deficit

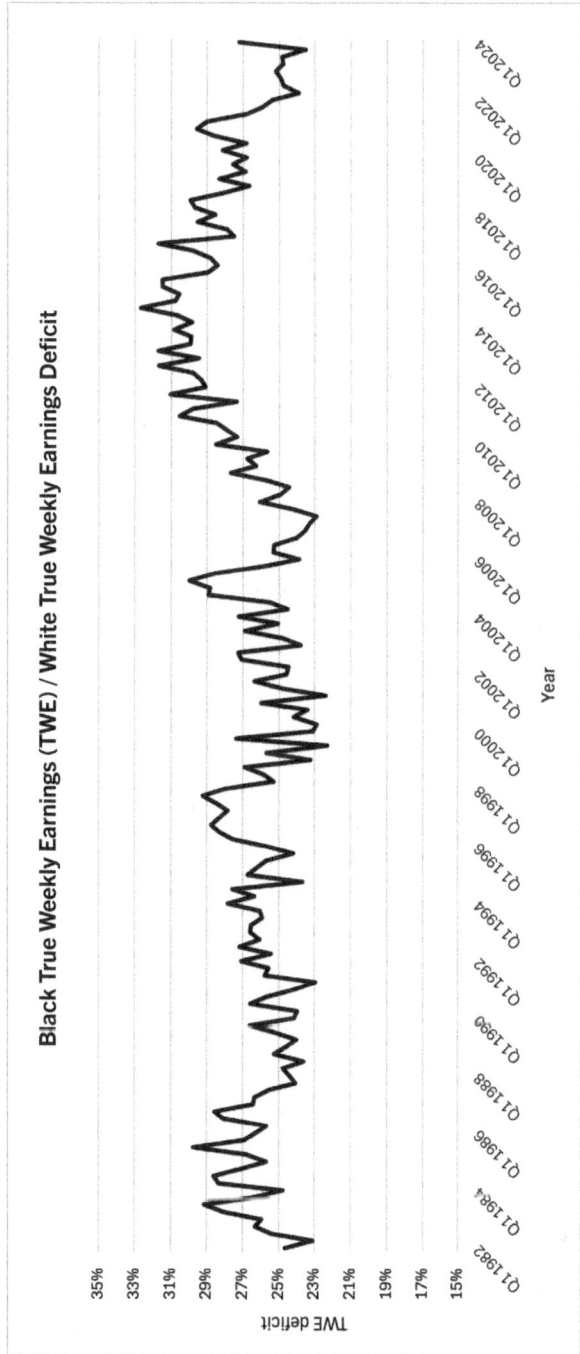

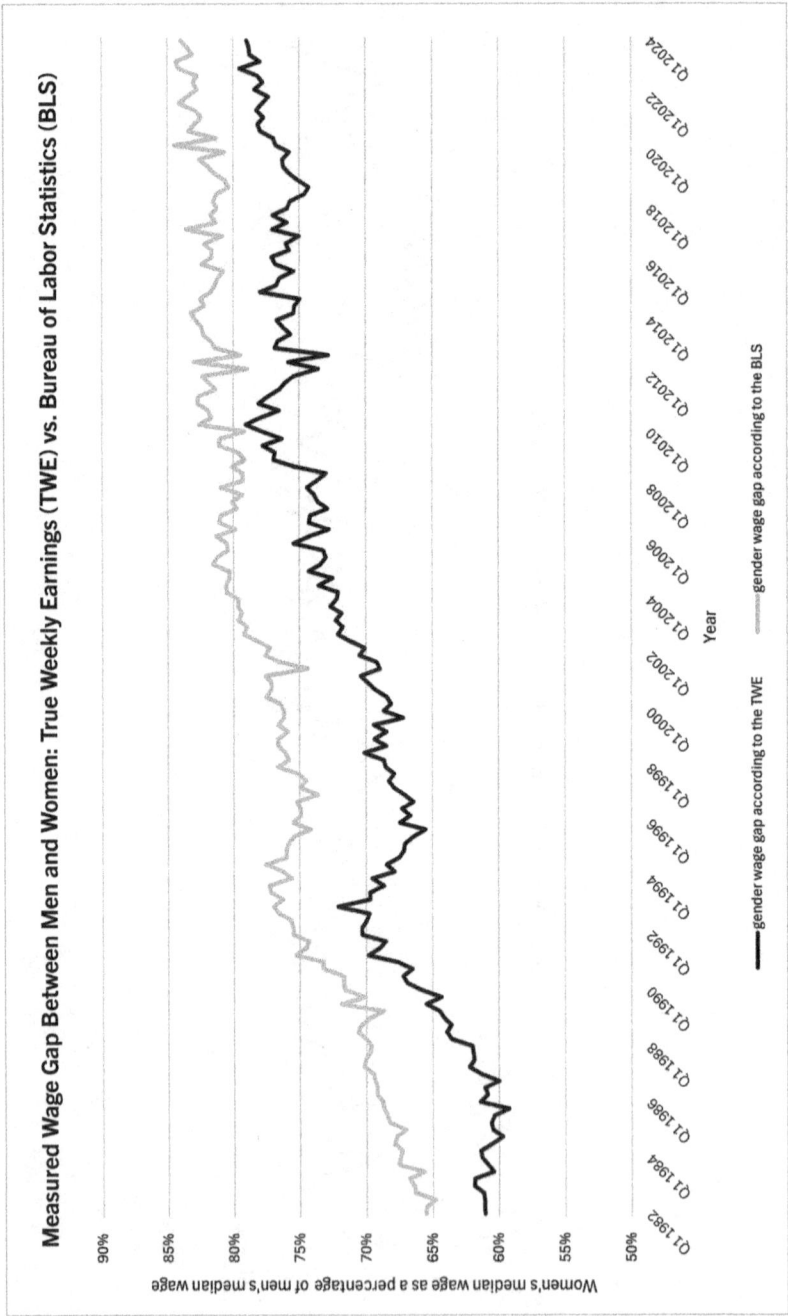

Measured Wage Gap Between Men and Women: True Weekly Earnings (TWE) vs. Bureau of Labor Statistics (BLS)

have wrung more stimulus out of Congress during the early months of the Great Recession and the ensuing slow expansion, sparking a swifter and stronger recovery. Perhaps efforts to narrow racial disparities would garner more political support today. Perhaps a clearer picture of reality would, in the end, point to a clearer path toward shared prosperity.

Regardless, what can't be denied is that the prevailing median-wage indicator pulls the wool over the eyes of those who need to understand how dreadfully the economy is serving broad swaths of the US population. As the previous chapter revealed, prevailing statistics work to blind everyone to the prevalence of *functional* unemployment. Here we can see that Americans aren't making nearly as much as statistics would tempt us to believe. And in the next chapter, we'll expose the truth about prices for the things low- and moderate-income Americans need to purchase—how they aren't as modest as we're typically told. And the upshot of *all* these misperceptions, taken together, is to desensitize us to the reality that the American Dream has been more elusive than is commonly understood.

Chapter 3

True Living Cost

HANGING ON BY OUR FINGERNAILS

When Brookings Institution scholar Dr. Isabel Sawhill endeavored, in 2018, to survey America's working class, she was struck by one woman's answer to a seemingly innocuous question: What economic class did the woman consider herself to be in? Middle class? Working class? The woman took a moment to think, and then responded: "I'm in the hanging-on-by-your-fingernails class."[1]

Whatever the prevailing "numbers" might have suggested—however good the economy might have been according to the statistics published in the newspaper—the woman's *personal* experience was akin to clinging to a thin rope-bridge above an abyss. From her vantage point, the American Dream must have appeared more like fantasy than reality. And as her comment made clear, she was frustrated, if not angry, about it.

When US policymakers have historically thought about the hanging-on-by-your-fingernails crowd, many likely imagined the nation's poor—families subsisting below the poverty line or in "deep poverty," a category that denotes a family living on income that is less than half of the poverty threshold.[2] Our collective impressions have been reflected elegantly and poignantly through the decades in Jacob Riis's photographs of the early twentieth century's Lower East Side, documentation of Robert Kennedy's famous tour of Appalachia, and the Baltimore neighborhoods depicted in *The Wire*. Our perception is born from an indisputable reality that the economically bereft in America are not really hanging on by their fingernails—many are barely hanging on at all.

But that sort of extreme and chronic poverty is not quite what the woman speaking to Dr. Sawhill meant. Her frustration was less about being poor and more about the serious pressure she felt she was under to *avoid* falling into actual poverty. It was about feeling that she was *downwardly mobile*—that no matter how hard she worked, no matter how much she scrounged, and no matter what she did, she viewed herself as incapable of maintaining her place on the economic ladder. She was what most of the world would consider working class,[i] but her grip on what has historically been a working-class lifestyle was slipping away.

What was so remarkable was that the woman's frustration was not reflected clearly, if at all, in the nation's economic indicators at the time. When Dr. Sawhill's important and thoughtfully constructed survey was being conducted, most analysts were bullish on the American economy. The recovery that followed the Great

---

i Although the woman's identity was not recorded, Dr. Sawhill's interviews focused on people who earned less than $70,000 a year, had no college degrees, and viewed themselves as positioned somewhere between "lower middle class" and "working class."

Recession marked the longest economic expansion in the nation's history.[3] By 2018, the S&P 500 wasn't just double what it had been in 2009—it had nearly tripled.[4] Yet, near the end of the recovery, nearly two in three lower-income adults still worried daily or almost daily about paying their bills.[5]

Months after the Covid-19 disruption, the market had recovered most of its value. Even so, by 2023, a full 72 percent of middle-income Americans reported feeling as though they were falling behind the cost of living.[6] A subsequent survey found that 66 percent of working-class voters reported that they were worse off than people like them forty years earlier, compared to the mere 21 percent who believed the working-class situation had improved.[7]

Why has economic *sentiment* diverged from what so many policymakers and economists believe to be economic *reality*? Why don't the tangible, day-to-day economic realities that many Americans face align with the prevailing headline statistics? Regardless of what the headline statistics so delphically portray, the empirical "facts on the ground" show that many Americans do not believe they're capable of providing for their children what their parents provided for them. They can't cover the costs of the same lifestyle that defined their own childhood—or, at least, not while maintaining the same work-life balance. The comforts that single-earner households could afford in, say, the 1970s appear in many cases to be inaccessible today, sometimes even for families with two breadwinners. That's not to suggest that everyone's financial situation has entirely failed to improve. Indeed, things have gotten better for certain slices of the economy and certain demographic groups. Since the Clinton administration, for example, child poverty has been cut by well more than half, due in large part to a range of specific policy programs, including the expansion of the Earned Income Tax Credit (EITC) and greater use of the Food Stamp Program now called the Supplemental Nutrition Assistance Program (SNAP).[8] (It bears pointing out that there are more than a few members of Congress who would roll back even these commendable advances.) And of course, financial markets have risen in value, with certain exceptions, creating enormous wealth for many Americans. But as the existence of the hanging-on-by-your-fingernails class proves, not *every* slice of the population—in fact, not even a majority of the population—has benefited. Too many Americans feel as though they're unable to come out ahead.[9]

As illustrated by the previous two chapters, certain statistics have duped policymakers into thinking things are better than they really are. Many more Americans are *functionally* unemployed than we tend to realize. Wages are, on the whole, more modest than the prevailing indicator suggests. But employment and income do not, by themselves, tell the whole story of economic well-being.

If price increases were more moderate than wage increases, life would then get cheaper and/or tangibly better in real terms. In this case, many working- and middle-class Americans would have reason to celebrate and be hopeful for a better future.

Some elements of this positive trajectory are visible in the not-so-distant past. At the turn of the twentieth century, improvements in public sanitation and plumbing, the expansion of the electrical grid, and advances in medicine all contributed to a sense that American life was generally getting better. The question is, does anything like that sense of promise still exist today? If, say, working-class incomes haven't risen as much as we presume, perhaps working-class lifestyles are less expensive. Perhaps a bounty of cheap goods coming from overseas, combined with the newfound prevalence of the digital economy—you couldn't stream movies at home twenty years ago—has made it easier to live a *better* life on a tightened budget. Whatever elements of reality might exist in these more recent developments, public impressions suggest things are actually fairly dire.

In March 2023, with the economy seemingly on a tear and the stock market well into a healthy recovery after the Covid-19 pandemic, only 12 percent of surveyed American adults reported that their economic situation was improving.[10] In the summer of that year, a survey of constituents in political battleground congressional districts found that 71 percent rated the economy as "poor" or "not so good."[11] Ultimately, then, the issue is how to square this circle—how to decipher whether there is more wisdom to be gleaned from the statistics or the polls.

Many living in a political and economic bubble have chosen to invest their faith in what appear, thanks to the nation's headline statistics, to be economic facts. They ascribe popular skepticism to cultural attitudes, insisting that Americans' economic concerns act as a thin veil for deep-seated racism and xenophobia.[12] When a national reporter stops into a local diner to take a measure of what's happening in a community, often they roll their proverbial eyes, concluding that complaints about the local mill closing are just a cover for the *real* reason they're angry.[13] And, in a few cases, no doubt, there's truth in that assessment.[14]

But in other cases—as we at LISEP believe, in *most* cases—the tendency to discount the testimonials about the financial struggles of middle- and lower-income Americans has gone too far. Since the pandemic, of course, inflation has been a centerpiece of economic reporting and broader discussions, dominated by rising prices for a range of consumer products and services. *Before* that, however, among the general public, discussions of price increases and inflation were few and far between.[15] The woman who told Dr. Sawhill she was hanging on by her fingernails offered her testimony *years* before the pandemic, at a point when the economy was purportedly humming. Perhaps, then, as in the cases of unemployment and wages, the headline statistics were—and still are—obscuring the truth.

By almost any standard, the federal government's approach to measuring inflation *appears* comprehensive. The Consumer Price Index for All Urban Consumers (CPI-U) gauges consumer prices in the 93 percent of the country that the Bureau of Labor Statistics considers "urban" (as determined by population counts).[ii] The CPI-U takes account of the prices charged for eighty thousand separate goods: apples, apartments, automobiles, smartphones, T-shirts, boats, and many, many more.[16] But because this basket of goods is so wide-ranging, there's real artistry to crafting the measure designed to reflect how "ordinary" consumers experience price changes in the aggregate. With any political poll, the sample matters. For example, a poll that overweighs Democrats or White voters or residents of Vermont would

---

ii Throughout this chapter, we will discuss the Consumer Price Index for All Urban Consumers (CPI-U) and the Consumer Price Index for Urban Wage Earners and Clerical Workers (CPI-W). The CPI-W covers a subset of the CPI-U population and is frequently used to adjust for cost of living, such as with Social Security payments. The CPI-U and the CPI-W are extremely similar as both track the same basket of eighty thousand goods and services with slightly different relative weights. Since both figures have been published starting in 1978, the CPI-U and the CPI-W have been correlated at more than 0.999 levels, based on author's calculations of US Bureau of Labor statistics. When discussing CPI as a concept, we use simply "CPI," meaning that the criticism applies to both of these headline CPI indexes.

likely give you a skewed understanding of broader political dynamics. The same is true for measuring prices—but as we'll see, the intricacies are vastly more complex.

If, for example, the costs of almost every consumer item stay flat during a set period while the cost of multimillion-dollar luxury yachts triples, the "ordinary" American household would be unlikely to feel much of a pinch—working-class households rarely purchase luxury yachts. The calculation therefore needs to somehow balance the impacts on the yacht-purchasing public and, well, everyone else. There is, of course, no perfect way to conjure the costs facing every individual American. Unfortunately, just as with the government's approach to calculating unemployment (chapter 1) and divining median wages (chapter 2), serious wrinkles in the methodology have profound impacts on the end result.

At a moment when the CPI plays such a powerful role in economic decision-making—shaping everything from social welfare thresholds to private-sector wages—we need to understand two things: one, how this key indicator illuminates the impacts price changes have on low- and middle-income Americans, and two, how it obscures other elements of their experience.[17] Does the most important measure of inflation give us an accurate picture of the prices that impact the average American's budget? Or, as we've discovered with other headline statistics, does the prevailing statistic shroud what's happening among less prosperous demographics?

A BURDEN (MIS)MEASURED

However useful it may be to conjure the image of the "average" American family, few will dispute that costs differ from one household to the next. It's not just that some households have the disposable income to purchase yachts while others struggle to afford basic necessities; it's that people with similar incomes living amid divergent circumstances are likely to purchase from different "baskets" of goods. Statisticians at the BLS are, of course, perfectly well aware of that. And, for that reason, the CPI-U strives to account for the costs shouldered by both rich and poor households alike. Unfortunately, however, the CPI-U does not provide any way of easily *disaggregating* those groups from the broader population.[18]

This is the core of the issue. As of the writing of this book, the BLS has only just begun to maintain a mechanism for separating the inflation that affects lower- and middle-class American households from price changes that affect those who live in luxury.[19] That limitation sparks frustration among those eager to understand discrete impacts on various demographics. It also hints at a related concern: In attempting to produce an aggregate measure of price changes faced by consumers up and down the economic ladder, the BLS has been compelled to craft a single indicator that strives to balance inflation across a whole range of different demographics.[20] That feature of the CPI-U has profound effects.

Just as it is possible that luxury yacht prices might rise more dramatically than the cost of essential items for working-class households— eggs, housing, or health care premiums, for example—the opposite can also be true. And if it *is* true, it means the relative stability of luxury items would mask the inflation faced by Americans of more modest means. Put simply, because the breadth of items included in the CPI-U's basket of goods is so immense, the CPI-U might do more to obscure the *true* cost of living for working-class Americans than it does to reveal it. And that is exactly what's happening.

Take, as an example, the way housing costs are factored into the CPI-U. The BLS tracks this by estimating a combination of prices for rental properties and owned properties, with the weight for each established by what a home *could* be rented for, even if the home is occupied by the owner; this statistic is known as the owners' equivalent rent of residences (OER). Because these prices come from a private database that the BLS does not make public, the housing figure is calculated using a different method from the rest of the CPI-U prices due to "less volatility" in housing prices. This different data collection method yielded a CPI-U for housing that rose 82 percent between 2001 and 2023.[21] Remarkably, however, home *values* rose much more dramatically during that same period—a full 170 percent, according to the renowned Case–Shiller Home Price Index.[22]

That's not to suggest the typical rents that working-class Americans pay have necessarily risen by 170 percent or, put another way, more than double the amount that the housing CPI-U suggests—rents and prices don't precisely align. But it does suggest that the housing and shelter CPI-U metrics may not be a particularly accurate gauge of how much money Americans have paid year-over-year for their housing costs. This statistical hiccup, of course, would distort the CPI-U more generally. And housing is just one among a litany of methodological concerns that point to a potential mismeasure of the cost concerns for working-class households.

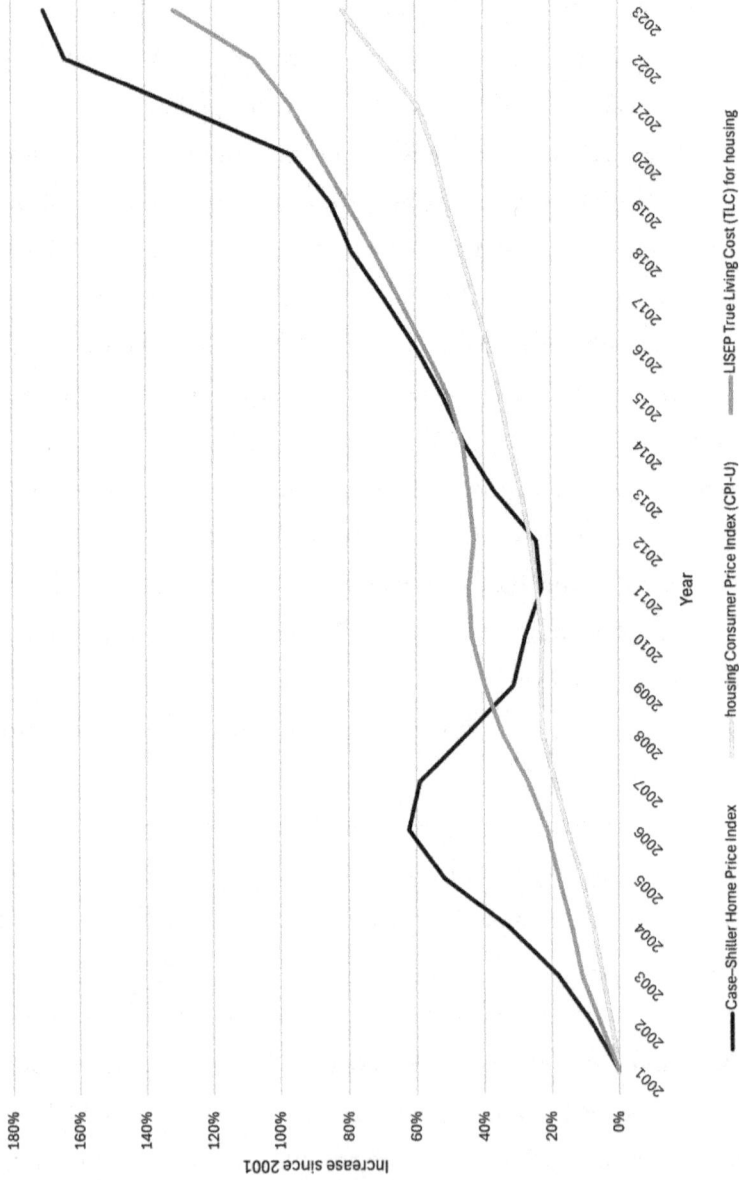

Housing Indexes Increase Since 2001

Increase since 2001

Year

——— Case-Shiller Home Price Index

··········· housing Consumer Price Index (CPI-U)

——— LISEP True Living Cost (TLC) for housing

When tracking health care costs, for example, BLS statisticians place great weight on the rates insurers charge health care providers for care. If a hospital implemented a 5 percent raise in the price it demands from an insurer for infant deliveries, and the insurer simultaneously hiked its premiums by 8 percent, the index would be affected more by the price paid to the hospital—the lower figure. Yet it's the higher figure—the premium—that actually impacts a family's budget. At a broader level, the fees that insurers pay to the providers have risen 114 percent since 2001.[23] But on the median, worker contributions to employer health care programs have risen 301 percent over the same period.[24] And the CPI-U is more influenced by the 114 percent hike than the 301 percent jump.[25]

Beyond incorporating stilted estimates in certain sectors including housing, the CPI-U often underweights cost considerations that apply primarily to households with more modest budgets. Consider mobile phone services, which were among the eighty thousand goods in the basket that was monitored thirty years ago—but not ubiquitous enough to have their own elementary-level price index as they had yet to become commonplace necessities.[iii] Today, by contrast, smartphones and wireless contracts are, for many Americans, indispensable—and often a prerequisite for jobs, if not more. But the CPI-U's methodology does not allow statisticians simply to add the cost of new technology to the index. Rather, weights are adjusted so they still sum to 100 percent, as though the old costs are somehow less of a burden now.

---

iii An elementary-level price index is the most granular index used to monitor specific goods and offers the most minute examination of price changes on a relatively homogenous group of products. They are published publicly for the Consumer Price Index by the BLS.

Consider how that works to distort reality: From year to year, Americans must cover certain costs—rent, gas, food, and electricity among them. When a *new* cost comes along, like those associated with owning a mobile telephone, the burden simply builds atop that foundation. Your rent doesn't diminish simply because you're compelled to sign a contract with a phone service provider. But the CPI-U, by formula, makes that implicit assumption, calculating that some portion of the *new* expense will be offset by savings elsewhere.[iv] In short, the prevailing measure of inflation shaves down the cost of new expenses as they accrue, distorting the real story—that the additional line item, in fact, just augments most households' cost burden.

Finally, and perhaps most disconcerting, the CPI-U is distorted by the way it weights various categories within its basket of eighty thousand goods and services. By dint of the underlying formula, the prices charged for watches and jewelry actually have more impact on the CPI-U than do the costs of rice and pasta, even though Americans living amid more modest circumstances are likely to buy only the latter.[26] Just as striking, the price for a *second* home has more weight than the prices charged for bread, pork, eggs, milk, chicken, and potatoes combined.[27]

This problem would not be so impactful if staple food items were inflating more modestly than the items consumed almost exclusively by those nearer the top of the economic ladder. But the opposite is true: Some prices for luxury items have grown much more modestly

---

iv Because the CPI uses a bundle that is determined by weights, the introduction of a new good necessarily would displace the importance of a different good, even if it's unrelated or not a substitute.

through the years.[v] Jewelry prices, for example, have risen in the CPI-U's measure by a mere 39 percent over the past twenty-two years, while bread became 112 percent more expensive and the cost of ground beef increased by 155 percent.[28]

For these three major reasons, any fair observer would have to be skeptical of whether the CPI-U is, in reality, a reliable indicator of cost of living. No single statistic could realistically claim to be a composite reflecting the reality for *all* households: Some are going to see the prices for their basket of costs rise more rapidly than others. And, in some cases, households with new financial burdens may be able to compensate by cutting back elsewhere. But the combined effect of these various hiccups is to distort the difference between economic classes. And, for that reason, it may well be that the sentiment expressed by many who *feel* downwardly mobile is a product of reality, not ignorance. In other words, we need to consider whether this important and leading indicator paints a distorted picture of what's really going on.

A STEEPER CLIMB

Is it possible to distill a clearer picture? Is there a better way to distinguish the statistical signals we get about working-class households from the noise created when tracking the population as a whole?

At its root, the CPI-U's shortcomings center primarily on its reliance on measures that, in too many cases, are too heavily weighted

---

v The problem is not only between luxury categories, though; it is also *within* categories. Transportation, for example, shows us that the prices of new cars have gone up 25.7 percent from 2001 to 2023 and the prices of used cars have gone up 20.5 percent. Airline prices, which are less impactful to the lower- and middle-income community than car prices (particularly used cars), have gone up only 11.6 percent in the same time frame.

to reflect the experience of those occupying the economic ladder's top rungs. If anyone wanted to understand the experience of, say, the woman who said she was hanging on by her fingernails, they would have to narrow their perspective to the goods and services that composed the bulk of her budget and measure more exclusively against those price changes. As discussed in the previous chapters, LISEP has endeavored to do exactly that: construct an alternative indicator that better tracks the experience of low- and middle-income Americans.

The first step in constructing this alternative measure, which LISEP has dubbed the True Living Cost (TLC), was to narrow the basket of indexed goods to a smaller subset of expenses the median working-class household can't go without.[29] In other words: Which goods and services are essential to those looking to maintain what LISEP researchers called a household's "minimal adequate needs"? Setting luxury goods and second homes aside, the TLC zeroes in on housing, food, transportation, health care, childcare, technology, and a collection of miscellaneous essentials (clothing, hygiene products, and the like). Thus, the TLC dispatches the most obvious problem with applying the CPI-U to measure the cost of living for low- and moderate-income Americans: namely, the potential distortion wrought by the reality that prices have risen more modestly for products and services geared toward those with more means.

Second, beyond narrowing the list of measured categories, LISEP reconsidered the price data used, knowing that lower- and middle-income households do not consume the same goods (or even the same goods within the same categories) that high-income households consume. Within the category of housing, for example, lower-income households are more likely to rent.[vi, 30] So, housing costs in the TLC are tied exclusively to a *rent* survey maintained by the US Department of Housing and Urban Development rather than to the OER. When measuring health care costs, LISEP chose to incorporate the costs borne by consumers rather than the costs charged by providers to insurance companies. As a result, we discovered that the combination of premiums and all out-of-pocket expenses paid by US consumers almost tripled between 2001 and 2022, whereas the costs paid by insurers had merely doubled.[31]

Finally, while the CPI-U presumes that new costs *replace* other expenses, the TLC recognizes that new categories will augment a household's financial burden. The TLC also incorporates the costs borne by the twenty-three million Americans living outside the urban areas from which the BLS derives its data for the CPI-U. LISEP also took care to account for different household arrangements.[32]

So, what did we find? First, and most important, the TLC tells a very different story than does the CPI-U. In fact, it gives almost immediate credence to US working-class perceptions of downward mobility.

---

vi Even so, a large minority of people in low-income households do own homes. LISEP didn't factor in a mortgage cost, however, for a few reasons: First, although a down payment and mortgage costs are indeed pricey, these are arguably investments rather than pure costs, because making these payments eventually leads to ownership of an asset (whereas rent payments are obviously just costs). Second, we wanted to take as conservative of an approach as possible, and rental payments are generally lower than the combination of a down payment, mortgage payments, and property taxes. As far as price inflation goes, we argue in the text that the Case–Shiller index outpaces both CPI-U housing and TLC housing (rents), so we are likely undershooting inflation for lower- and middle-income Americans. Finally, the trajectory of homeownership among all age groups currently is moving lower; see "Consumer Unit Characteristics: Percent Homeowner by Age: from Age 25 to 34 (CXUHOMEOWNLB0403M)," BLS via Federal Reserve Bank of St. Louis, accessed February 9, 2025, https://fred.stlouisfed.org/series/CXUHOMEOWNLB0403M.

Between 2001 and 2023, the CPI-U rose by 72.1 percent, or, on average, 2.5 percent a year. In other words, a household's income needed to grow in the aggregate by roughly two-thirds to maintain a consistent lifestyle. According to the CPI-U, a household spending $50,000 in 2001 would have to spend slightly more than $86,000 in 2023 to afford the same panoply of goods and services. This was considered tame in the scheme of price increases—nothing to spark widespread alarm.[vii]

Rarely during these years did anyone pay any particular mind to inflation. Admittedly, the Fed increased the federal funds rate between 2004 and 2006 because of its concerns about inflation. Moreover, even amid the easy fiscal and monetary policy and the near-zero rate policies pursued during the Great Recession and the ensuing sluggish recovery years, Federal Open Market Committee (FOMC) members and other policymakers in Washington expressed concerns about the potential inflationary effects.[33] But inflation was not as important of an issue for policymakers and the media as it was during the 1970s and 1980s. In general little attention was paid to the changing reality for low- and middle-income Americans. Rising prices were, for many, an economic afterthought.

If inflation really had been limited to a manageable 2.5 percent per year, that lack of attention would perhaps have been justified. But the TLC paints a very different picture, suggesting the 2.5 percent figure did not reflect reality for many slices of the American demographic pie.

---

vii In fact, the 2.5 percent inflation rate is consistent with the Federal Reserve's long-run inflation target of 2 percent. The Fed has aimed toward this behind the scenes since 1996 and publicly since 2012. Matthew Wells, "The Origins of the 2 Percent Inflation Target," Federal Reserve Bank of Richmond, 2024, https://www.richmondfed.org/publications/research/econ_focus/2024/q1_q2_federal_reserve.

Here's what may be the most startling statistic to come from the TLC: For lower- and middle-class Americans, prices didn't rise a mere 72.1 percent as the CPI-U would have us believe. They jumped by 97.4 percent—that's 35.1 percent more than what was reported.[34] So, a household spending $50,000 in 2001 wouldn't have needed $86,000 (as the CPI-U indicated) to maintain the same lifestyle in 2023—they would, in fact, have required $98,700 to keep pace. Absent that sort of bump in their earnings, they would have felt as though they were falling behind. And they would have been right.

In the following chapter, we will explore in greater depth how inflation has affected the US consumer's "purchasing power." But it's worth pausing here to note the distinct trajectories of (1) median wages and (2) the costs required to fulfill a household's minimal adequate needs. Between 2001 and 2023, registered nurses saw their median incomes grow 81 percent. Those working as auto mechanics saw their incomes rise 82 percent. Firefighters saw their incomes rise 55 percent.[35] And as the CPI-U rose a mere 72.1 percent during this period, it might *appear*, on paper, that these rising incomes would have covered most of whatever costs were born from ordinary inflation. But as the TLC reveals, prices *actually* rose by 97.4 percent. So, the typical middle-class worker was, in fact, downwardly mobile.

A TALE OF DOWNWARD MOBILITY

Higher costs affect different Americans in different ways over time. Some Americans making lower- or middle-class wages in 2001 have since stepped into more prosperous circumstances: Mom got a promotion.

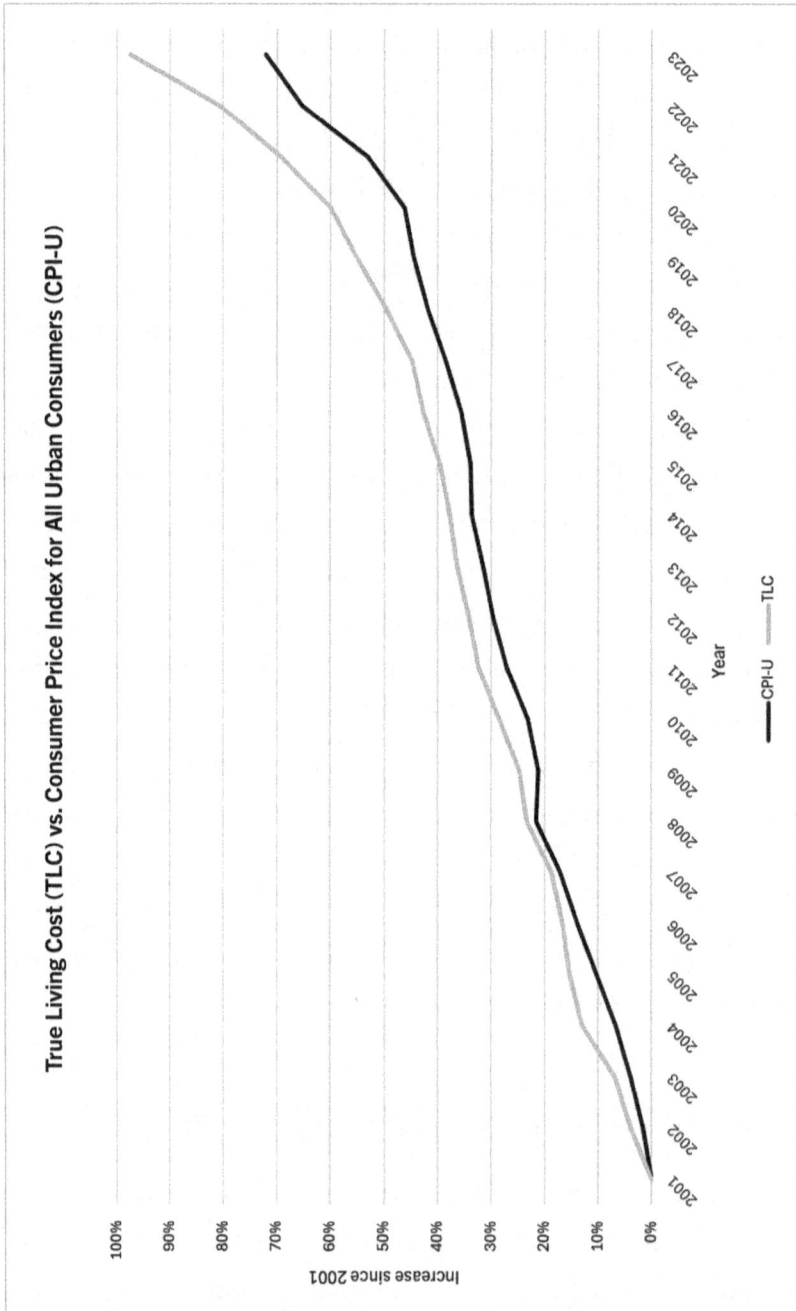

True Living Cost (TLC) vs. Consumer Price Index for All Urban Consumers (CPI-U)

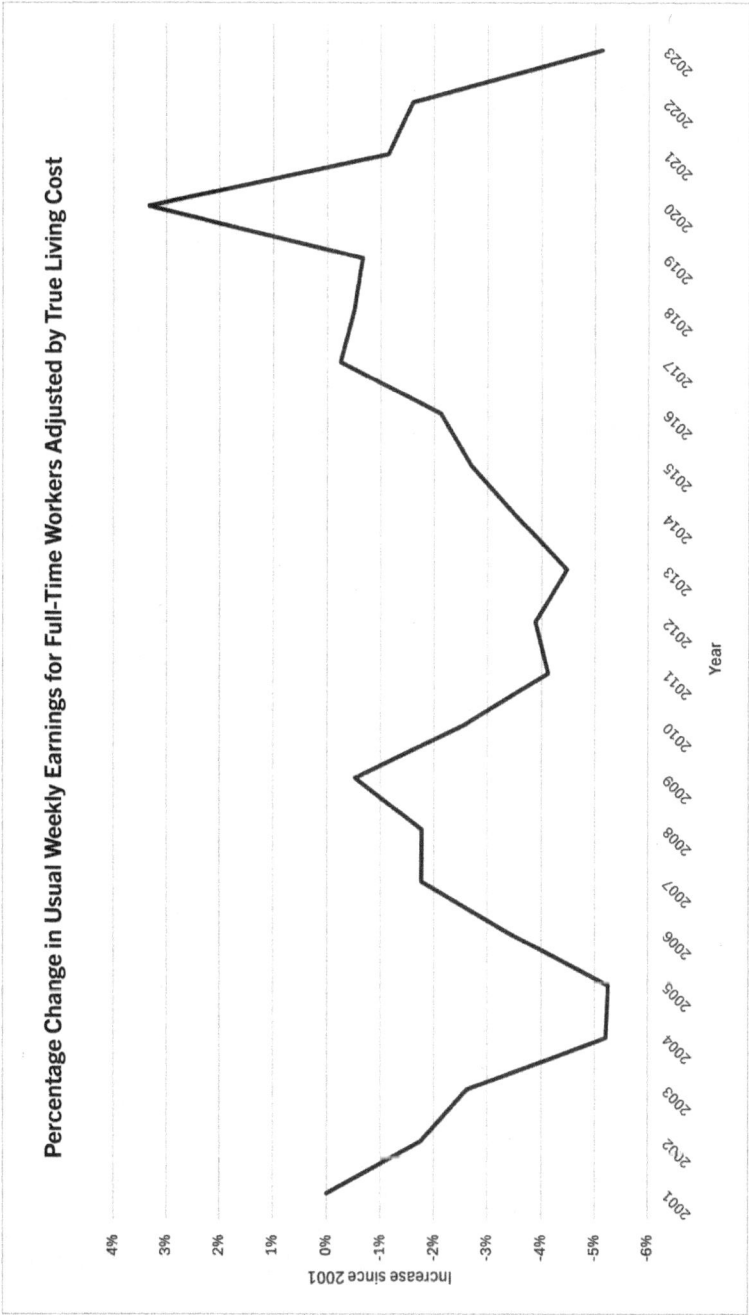

Percentage Change in Usual Weekly Earnings for Full-Time Workers Adjusted by True Living Cost

Dad changed careers. The family moved to a less expensive locale. When trying to understand any individual person's economic mobility, it's hard to isolate price inflation from other factors like these. But at least one demographic serves as a near-perfect petri dish for examining the impact of inflation: retirees with pensions.

To be sure, "pensioners" aren't as prevalent today as they were during the postwar era. A smaller percentage of today's American workers are entitled to what are now known as "defined benefit" pensions.[36] But most readers will nevertheless be familiar with the underlying arrangement: To induce employees to stay for the long haul—to incentivize their loyalty—companies can offer access to a pension fund, controlled either by the company or, in some cases, by a union. Money invested in that fund is provided later as an annual disbursement to the employee (or the employee's spouse) during his or her retirement.[37] The disbursement grows at set amounts throughout the time when they collect benefits, often in increments that correspond to the CPI.[viii] Tracking their experiences can thus illuminate the reality that the TLC is designed to expose.

The pension system's appeal was clear: If you intended to spend, say, thirty years working for the same company, you need not worry about siphoning off portions of your monthly income for retirement—the pension would provide. Perhaps even better, through what were commonly termed "Cost of Living Adjustments," or COLAs, your benefits would rise with inflation over time. If a pension

---

viii Specifically, the price change used to adjust pension payments is the Consumer Price Index for Urban Wage Earners and Clerical Workers (CPI-W). Given their similar design, the CPI-W (which increased 72.3 percent between 2001 and 2023) follows a very similar trajectory to the CPI-U.

afforded a retired couple enough to maintain a certain lifestyle at the beginning of their retirement, the theory went, it would empower them to afford the same lifestyle nearer the end.

Fewer companies today offer defined benefit pensions in large part because (as discussed in previous chapters) fewer employers are motivated to elicit long-term loyalty. Nevertheless, in 2023, a full 19 percent of the civilian labor force—more than thirty million workers—were contributing to defined benefit pensions, including about three-quarters of the nation's teachers (72 percent, to be exact), nearly half of the workers engaged in protective service occupations (law enforcement, firefighters, and so forth—46 percent), and roughly a quarter of the nation's nurses (26 percent).[38]

For the purposes of our understanding the impact of inflation, the crucial question is: Are pension benefits, many of which were tied to inflation through CPI-adjusted COLAs, keeping up with the recipients' *actual* cost of living? Consider, as a single sample group among those who receive defined pensions, the nation's veterans. Provided a US soldier has accrued at least twenty years of service, retirees are entitled to a military pension. Many of them surely presume that the payout they receive on a monthly basis, adjusted periodically to keep up with the CPI, will empower them to maintain the same lifestyle through the course of their retirements. But as our research uncovered, veterans in 2024 were earning 12.5 percent less than they would have received if their benefits had been tied to the TLC rather than the Consumer Price Index for Urban Wage Earners and Clerical Workers (CPI-W). For those who had been retired since 2002, the accumulated shortfall represented nearly $46,000.

This shortfall is directly tied to the methodological issues described

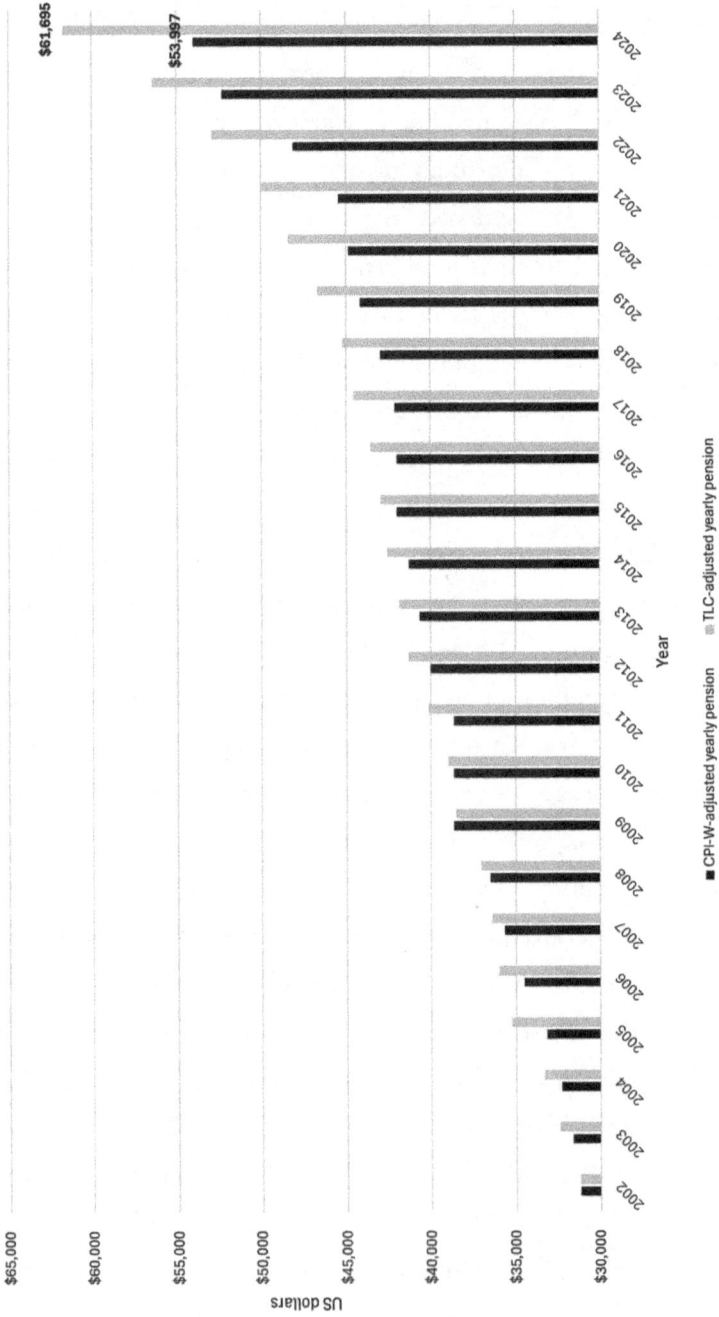

Consumer Price Index for Urban Wage Earners and Clerical Workers (CPI-W)-Adjusted Yearly Pension vs. True Living Cost (TLC)-Adjusted Yearly Pension for a Master Sergeant

above: The CPI-W does not rise in tandem with the costs of meeting a working-class or military worker's minimal adequate needs. In 2002, for example, the military pension of a master sergeant who retired a year earlier with thirty years of service was about $2,600 per month—the equivalent of $31,200 per year.[39] Adjusted by the CPI-W, twenty-two years later that pension paid out slightly less than $54,000. But because the costs of ordinary items had gone up much more steeply, in 2024 that $54,000 would not have covered what $31,200 would have covered in 2002. To keep parity, the 2024 payment would have needed to grow to $61,700, per the TLC.[40] As grateful as many veterans might be for having a continuing source of income, many surely have noted that as they grow older, they are falling behind.

KEEPING PACE

Like the prevailing indicators for unemployment and median wages, the CPI undoubtedly has a *soft* impact on the economy by shaping broader perceptions of the nation's prosperity. If the CPI-U is rising dramatically, for example, many presume ordinary people are *feeling* poorer—and in many cases, that's true. But in contrast to other economic indicators, the CPI-U and the CPI-W have a harder impact as well.

For one, as we saw above, the benefits a pensioner receives are typically tied to the CPI-W. But it's not just pensions. The government's prevailing measure of inflation directly impacts a whole range of other public policies and private-sector decision-making. Indeed, the CPI's distortions ripple out in profound ways that are perhaps unintended—but malign nonetheless.

Percentage Contributing to Defined Benefit Pension Plans by Occupational Group: All Civilian Workers

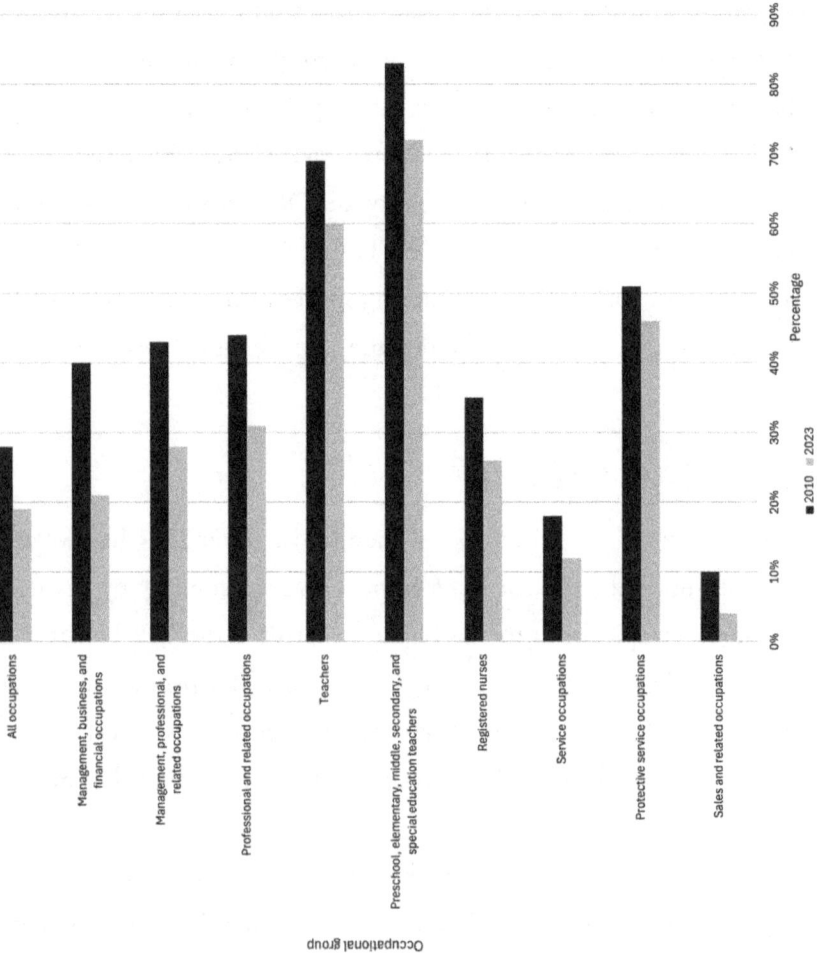

Percentage Contributing to Defined Benefit Pension Plans by Occupational Group: All Civilian Workers (cont.)

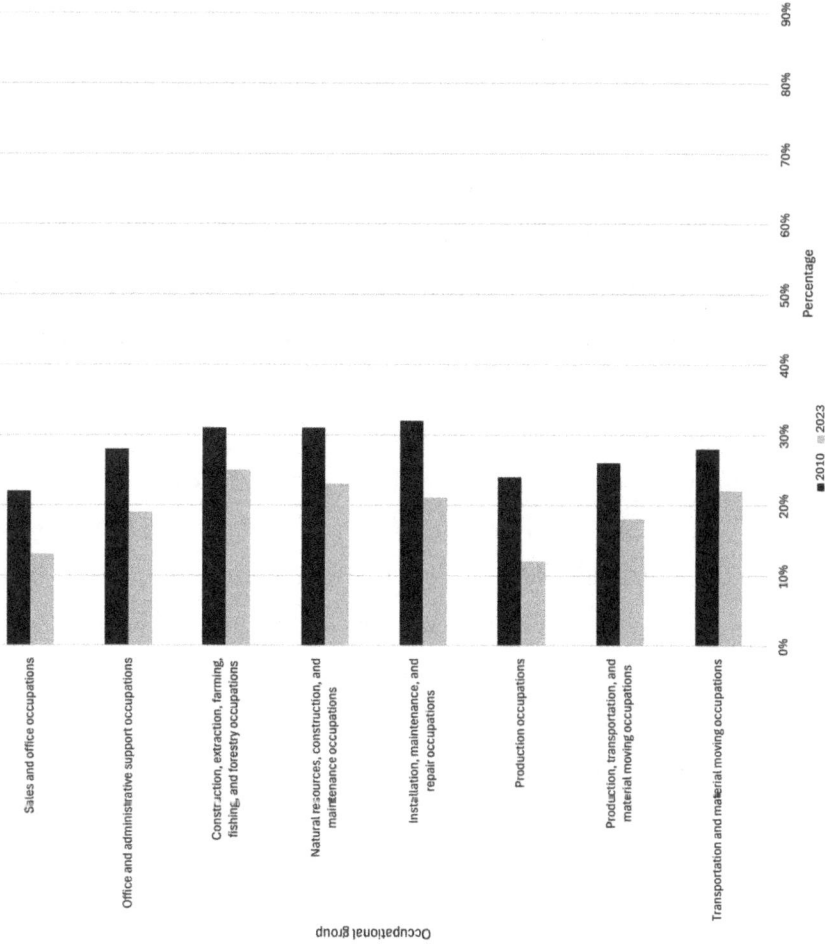

Occupational group

Sales and office occupations

Office and administrative support occupations

Construction, extraction, farming, fishing, and forestry occupations

Natural resources, construction, and maintenance occupations

Installation, maintenance, and repair occupations

Production occupations

Production, transportation, and material moving occupations

Transportation and material moving occupations

Percentage

■ 2010 ■ 2023

The foundation of the American social safety net—Social Security—offers the clearest illustration of the CPI's influence. Social Security was designed to work something like the pensions described above: Workers pay into the system throughout their careers in order to earn certain defined benefits in retirement.[41] The details differ in some respects, but the basic model is the same: If you qualify, you are guaranteed some level of income throughout your "golden years."[42]

As with pensions, the benefits retirees receive from Social Security are established on a start date and adjusted through the years. These COLAs, tied directly to the CPI-W, are made for the same underlying reason: As the cost of groceries rises, so, in theory, should the size of a recipient's benefit check. If the CPI-W rises by 2 percent in a given year, benefit checks are mandated to rise by a commensurate amount.[ix] And the bumps compound. If a retiree was due to receive $20,000 from Social Security in one year, and the CPI-W rises 2 percent that year, they'd subsequently receive $20,400 the following year. If the CPI-W rises 2.5 percent that second year, the retiree's benefit would then be calculated against the $20,400 annual benefit. And so, in the third year, the retiree would be due $20,910.

But if, as we've established, the CPI-W understates inflation for the majority of Americans—if, in fact, costs for lower- and middle-class retirees are rising more rapidly than the CPI-W would suggest—the

---

ix More precisely, the COLA is equivalent to the third-quarter, year-over-year percentage change in CPI-W, rounded to the nearest tenth of a percent. For example, 2024's 3.2 percent COLA corresponded to the percentage change in the third quarter's average of the nonseasonal CPI-W between 2022 and 2023. "Fact Sheet: Social Security," Social Security Administration, accessed February 9, 2025, https://www.ssa.gov/news/press/factsheets/colafacts2024.pdf; "Cost-of-Living Adjustment (COLA) Information for 2025," Social Security Administration, accessed February 9, 2025, https://www.ssa.gov/cola/#:~:text=Thepercent20CPIpercent2DWpercent20ispercent20 determined,annualpercent20COLAspercent20beganpercent20inpercent201975.

compounding effect works counterintuitively to ensure those receiving benefits fall further behind each successive year.

For example, someone who retired at age sixty-five in 2002 might have been granted monthly benefits that accrued to $10,000 for the year. Because the CPI-W was determined to have risen 1.4 percent in 2002, their benefit would have risen to $10,140 in their second year. Because the CPI-W was 2.1 percent in 2003, their benefit would have risen to $10,353 in 2004. But of course, for all the reasons explained above, $10,353 would not have covered the same universe of goods and services in 2004 as $10,000 would have covered in 2002.

The difference on the margin between 2002 and 2004 might not seem to be of any great significance, but the compounding effect slowly levers the disparity. By 2024, the recipient's benefit would have risen by roughly 73.1 percent per the CPI-W, while the cost of resources required to meet the beneficiary's minimal adequate needs would have risen by more than 97.4 percent. And the ensuing delta represents an inevitable turn toward downward mobility.

By 2024, the recipient's benefits would have grown to $17,307 per year based on the CPI-W. Had the TLC been the prevailing metric, the figure would have been $19,774. That's a difference of 14.3 percent, or $2,400.[43] And for most American retirees, particularly those in the working class and middle class, the extra money would have marked a sizable improvement in their situation.

If Social Security has the broadest reach, a range of other US government programs are similarly tied to the CPI-U. Inflation bears directly on poverty thresholds, which are determined by the Census Bureau. If costs rise, the upper limits of eligibility are supposed to rise with them. And a whole range of safety net benefits—SNAP;

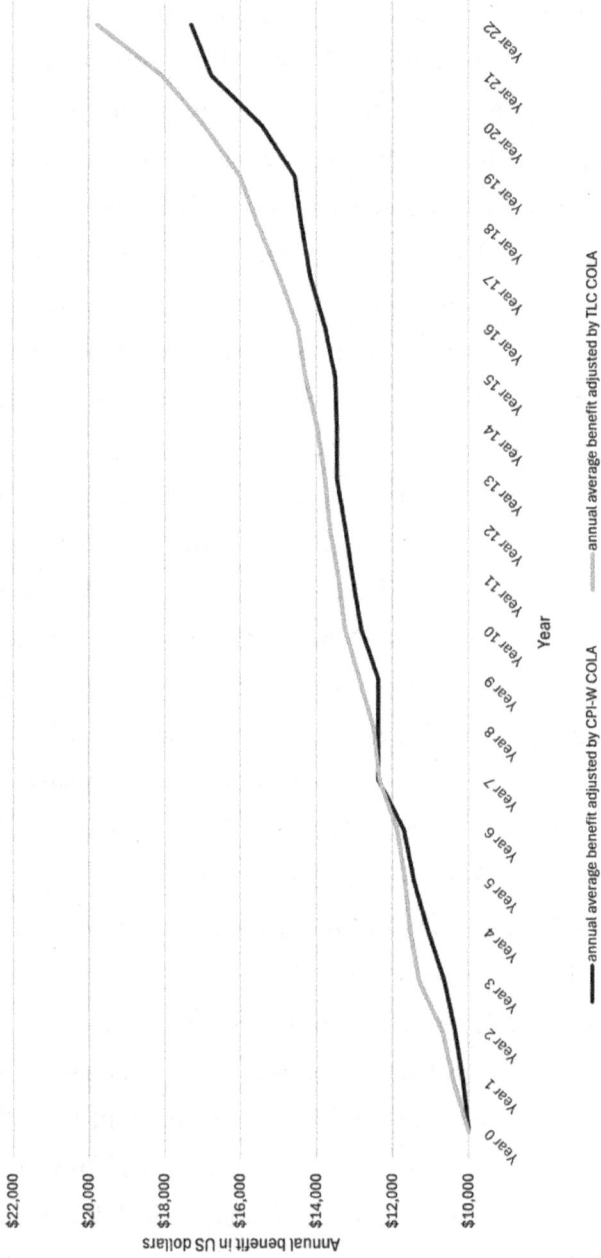

True Living Cost-Adjusted Social Security Benefits vs. Consumer Price Index for Urban Wage Earners and Clerical Workers-Adjusted Social Security Benefits

Based on December 2002 Average Benefit

Head Start; Pell Grants; and the Children's Health Insurance Program (CHIP), which covers kids above the income cutoff for Medicaid—are limited to households that earn below a certain income limit, which is based on the poverty line.[44]

But when the thresholds don't rise in step with minimal adequate needs, many who *should* qualify for the social programs—Americans the programs were designed to serve—are deemed ineligible. That is, people who would have qualified if threshold increases accurately reflected rises in cost of living are excluded from receiving benefits. If thresholds were raised in line with the TLC, millions of additional Americans—those making as much as 14 percent more than today's cutoff—would still be below the poverty threshold. Put another way, if the poverty threshold had risen since 2001 with the TLC rather than the CPI-U, seven million additional Americans in 2023 would have been considered living in poverty.[45]

The table on the following page reveals what the poverty lines would be for each household size in 2024 if, each year since 2001, Washington had adjusted the poverty thresholds according to the TLC instead of the CPI-U.[x]

---

x Poverty guidelines as published by the Department of Health and Human Services. See "Prior HHS Poverty Guidelines and Federal Register References," Office of the Assistant Secretary for Planning and Evaluation, accessed February 9, 2025, https://aspe.hhs.gov/topics/poverty -economic-mobility/poverty-guidelines/prior-hhs-poverty-guidelines-federal-register-references.

2024 published vs. True Living Cost-adjusted poverty guidelines

Household size	Headline poverty line (HHS)	True Living Cost poverty line	Absolute difference	% difference
1	$15,060	$17,510	$2,450	16.3
2	$20,440	$23,590	$3,150	15.4
3	$25,820	$29,670	$3,850	14.9
4	$31,200	$35,750	$4,550	14.6
5	$36,580	$41,830	$5,250	14.4
6	$41,960	$47,910	$5,950	14.2
7	$47,340	$53,990	$6,650	14.0
8	$52,720	$60,070	$7,350	13.9

Finally, the CPI has a direct impact on private-sector wages. At least twelve states and the District of Columbia index their minimum wages to the CPI.[46] And for the same reason that pensioners and recipients of Social Security fall behind on minimal adequate needs, this purportedly progressive impulse leaves private-sector employees functionally poorer year after year. Ohio's minimum wage, for example, rose from $6.85 per hour in 2007 to $10.45 in 2024, in line with the CPI-W. But if it had been indexed to the TLC, the minimum wage in 2024 would have been $11.50 per hour. For a typical person working fifty-two weeks per year and forty hours per week, that translates to earning over $2,184 more per year—a big hike when you're only making $21,736 a year.[47]

But the mismeasure extends well beyond those earning a minimum wage. In many cases, labor unions bargain to ensure their wages are indexed to the CPI, such that a laborer scheduled to make a certain figure during the first year of a contract will automatically make more the second year, and so on.[48] But, again, if the CPI fails to capture the costs endured by lower- and middle-class workers, even these purportedly far-sighted union contracts leave wage earners to suffer diminished purchasing power—they become, almost by definition, downwardly mobile.

PROFOUND COSTS

There is no mystery as to why the prevailing measures of unemployment and median wages, examined in the previous two chapters, spur frustration among the general public: In one case, people who are *functionally* unemployed aren't counted among those struggling to find work. In the other, prompted by public reporting, people who believe wages are rising during downturns are subsequently made to feel as though they're falling behind. In both cases, broad perceptions do not track with the prevailing statistics. And, so, the discourse among economic policymakers becomes increasingly disconnected from the realities that low- and middle-income Americans face every day.

By focusing on the true cost of living, we can see how the distortions wrought by our mismeasure of price increases play much the same role, as the public has endured decades of inflation shrouded by the leading indicator. But in this case, the effects are more direct because the CPI's shortcomings are a source of material deprivation, effectively funneling downward mobility. This misapplied metric deprives pensioners of the ability to maintain their lifestyles through retirement. It deprives recipients of Social Security of the benefits that would keep them at par. It excludes people who *should* qualify for public benefits from receiving them. And it even depresses private-sector compensation for whole swaths of the workforce.

The broader policy implications that could be born from replacing the CPI as a cost-of-living measure with the TLC are profound. Government expenditures would surely rise. Private-sector labor costs would grow. More Americans would be able to draw down from public coffers. And those changes would likely have profound fiscal and political effects. Policymakers would need to determine how to navigate the fallout. Would the government find new sources of revenue to fill any budget gap? Would other expenditures need to be cut? Would various programs need to be molded in ways to direct more limited resources to the worthiest efforts? Navigating that fallout would be complex, but at least policymakers would be facing economic reality for the American people as it truly exists.

The woman who told Dr. Sawhill she felt as though she was hanging on by her fingernails was expressing a reality that is borne out in real life—even if the truth is hidden by the prevailing statistics: The cost of living is rising faster than the jobs and resources available to low- and middle-income Americans. It has become *de rigeur* for Washington insiders to rue America's declining faith in institutions of all kinds—government among them.[49] Yet here, in bright contrast, is an eminently plausible reason why: Many Americans *are* downwardly mobile, despite the economic metrics failing to register their lived experience. And the CPI has not only blinded many economic decision-makers to reality—Washington's reliance on this single misguided economic indicator also almost undoubtedly makes working-class lives materially more difficult.

Chapter 4

Shared Economic Prosperity

AMERICAN DREAMS AND UPWARD MOBILITY

The previous three chapters focused on more reliable and objective measures of the American economy—the ways we gauge unemployment, earnings, and the cost of living. As we have seen, the existing headline indicators in these areas produce a distorted view of the economy, failing to illuminate the decline in the well-being of large segments of our population: More people are functionally unemployed than anyone would realize when reading the headline unemployment statistic, the U-3, or even the less common but more comprehensive U-6. Wages are more modest than anyone would realize if they tracked the incumbent indicator measuring median earnings. And middle- and low-income Americans have suffered more from price increases than anyone would presume when faced with the prevailing measures of inflation. Indeed, these three headline statistics we have reviewed almost unfailingly overstate the well-being of low- and middle-income Americans.

LISEP's indicators offer a more nuanced perspective on economic reality, painting a picture more reflective of reality on the ground— one that is better aligned with the everyday experiences in many, if not all, American cities and towns. But even LISEP's indicators do not fully illuminate the scope of the challenges and ugliness many of our fellow citizens are facing. The vast discrepancy between reported and actual realities has created significant psychological and social burdens that deserve further exploration.

To begin with, the discrepancy between perception and reality erodes faith in government. It strains credibility when federal policy-makers boast a rising GDP while homeless encampments exist right under their noses in Washington, DC. Similarly, the economic statistics, while acknowledging the economic slide for middle- and low-income Americans, fail to capture the individual citizen's gnawing sense of decline. Americans, encouraged from on high to believe what they read rather than what they experience, are also losing faith in the hope historically contained in the American Dream.

One way we can glean a clearer picture of twenty-first-century American economic reality—and the potential dangers ahead—is by examining the widening chasm that has emerged as the American economy has grown. Top incomes have risen while a majority of Americans have struggled to stay afloat. Looking across this chasm, more accurate statistics reveal how economic well-being has moved beyond the grasp of the vast majority of Americans—this latter, huge group made up largely of individuals in the hanging-on-by-their-fingernails class is struggling to maintain a decent standard of living. And that raises a critical question: What will it take economically to revitalize the American Dream for the less advantaged 60 percent of our society?

The constituent elements of the American Dream are not, of course, inscribed in any legal document. This *beau ideal* can't be reduced to a white picket fence, or "a chicken in every pot," or a single-family home in the suburbs. The American Dream is more dynamic than that. It's the desire that most parents hold: that with hard work and gumption, their children will be able to do a bit better than the generation that came before them.

The *presumption* of upward mobility has long distinguished American life, most pointedly differentiating this nation from the places immigrants and migrants have come *from*—economies where families could only hope, at best, to maintain their place through the generations. Freed to make the most of their talent and savvy, many Americans have been taught to believe that simply by dint of living in this society, they hold license to climb the ladder of prosperity. For much of the nineteenth and twentieth centuries, Americans who worked hard and played by the rules were able to make good on that bargain, however unevenly. The sectors that prevailed, and the arrangements employers maintained with the workforce, put generational improvement within the grasp of millions of Americans.

In 1950, 31 percent of the nation's nonfarm workforce was employed in manufacturing, making it a paragon for middle-class prosperity.[1] The postwar era was far from the best of all possible worlds, as many wanted to believe. Those decades were rife with racism, sexism, xenophobia, and more. Women were often precluded from working outside the home. Minorities were often denied basic rights, privileges, and opportunities. Manufacturing might have offered stable, better-paying jobs, but discrimination in both private employment and government policy limited its benefits. Political compromises, like the Federal Housing Administration's enforcement of loan segregation, locked many people out of homeownership and the middle-class security it promised.[2] In many ways, the system was deeply flawed. Yet, despite these inequities, the postwar manufacturing sector boasted something remarkable and increasingly rare: jobs that made it possible for single-breadwinner families—even for those who had not completed high school—to afford a middle-class lifestyle.[3] With that came a sense of dynamic optimism—a notion that opportunity was abundant.

With a steady job in manufacturing, households could often afford to meet their needs, build a better future, and even enjoy a few luxuries. Families started sending their children to college at unprecedented rates.[4] In essence, however generous or meager they were in real terms, prevailing incomes represented the promise of upward mobility. In communities ranging from the rolling hills of Amish country Pennsylvania to the flat, productive plains of the Midwest to the ranches and lush river valleys of the far West, this engendered not just a sense of life getting *better* but a notion of a better life being *earned.*

To be sure, upward mobility often came with strings attached. For those employed in the industrial sector, upward trajectories often required a certain long-term relationship between business and labor. Many, if not most, Americans riding this particular escalator intuitively understood that they were entering a social contract designed to balance the demands of the nation's employers, the nation's employees, and the government. But the bargain largely seemed fair: If a worker contributed their toil, they could presume that their job would remain theirs from year to year, that their salary would grow, and that they would be able to afford a comfortable home, a family car, a television, and a yearly vacation. They could expect that their pension would take care of their retirement and their employer-subsidized health insurance would cover their family's medical expenses.[5] And they could anticipate that some diligence would put higher education within reach for their children.[6] This was the foundation on which postwar parents bequeathed upward mobility to the baby boomers.

To the degree this book has focused on specific economic metrics, it's important now to understand that these figures combine to establish something more than a statistical abstract. The headline statistics of those decades girded the foundation of a narrative that members of the workforce understood and embraced. Of the children born in 1940, 90 percent would grow up to earn more than their parents.[7] *That* was the promise of American life in the 1950s and 1960s. *That* was the American Dream. *That* was the nation's hope for the future. And the question today is, does that hope still prevail? Perhaps more pointedly, is the American Dream warranted by economic reality?

DECOUPLING GROWTH AND OVERALL PROSPERITY

The American Dream that framed life during the postwar era was girded by a central pillar: sustained growth. Market economies are cyclical, of course, so America's prosperity took a few hits. The country endured four mild recessions in the eighteen years spanning the end of World War II and the JFK assassination. Indeed, in the months before President Kennedy's fateful trip to Dallas, he had worried about "excessive unemployment, unused capacity, and slack profits."[8] Nevertheless, America throughout this era embraced a widely accepted notion that a stable industrial economy, buffeted by what the eminent economist John Kenneth Galbraith termed "countervailing forces," might grow forever.[i] America's inflation-adjusted gross national product (called "real GNP"), a statistic designed to measure the *size* of an economy, doubled in less than twenty years.[9]

Some portion of that growth was fueled by government spending in areas such as the construction of the interstate system, the military buildup fueled by the Cold War, and the production of American products to meet the demands of consumers in beleaguered parts of the war-torn world. But the nation's affluence was bigger than that. New consumer products came online that made life easier and seemingly better: affordable homes, appliances, televisions, cars, and more. Prosperity appeared to be on the march. And the feeling of potentially permanent growth was coupled with something else—a notion that everyone was poised to benefit *together*.[10]

When building public support for his economic program, Kennedy coined an iconic phrase: "A rising tide," he argued, "lifts all boats."[11] That hadn't been true during the Gilded Age or even during the Roaring Twenties that preceded the Great Depression. Back then, the rich had appeared to leave others behind. But now, the president

---

i In his 1952 book *American Capitalism*, Galbraith "described the pressures that corporations and unions exerted on each other for increased profits and increased wages, and said these countervailing forces kept those giant groups in equilibrium and the nation's economy prosperous and stable." See "John Kenneth Galbraith, 97, Dies; Economist Held a Mirror to Society," *The New York Times*, April 30, 2006, https://www.nytimes.com/2006/04/30/obituaries/john-kenneth-galbraith-97-dies-economist-held-a-mirror-to.html.

argued, Americans could finally climb the economic ladder to opportunity in earnest. On the eve of World War I, the richest 1 percent of the population had claimed as much as one-fifth of the nation's income—but by 1970, that had fallen in many places to one-tenth or less. Perhaps more remarkably, between 1950 and 1970, adults in the bottom 50 percent saw their pretax income double on average, while people in the top 5 percent saw theirs grow a mere 32 percent.[12] The income gap, by these measures, was indeed shrinking.

Income inequality, of course, is not a perfect proxy for upward mobility. The income gap between CEOs and people in the working class can increase, in theory, even as everyone climbs up the economic ladder. But during the period when people *felt* that the rising tide was lifting all boats, the two ideas were aligned: Improved salaries nearer the bottom of the income scale chipped away at the disparity separating wealthier and more workaday communities. Those working in finance saw an average real-wage gain of 21 percent between 1951 and 1979. Those working in durable goods, by contrast, saw a 47 percent wage gain, while those in "special trades" saw their wages grow by 36.4 percent.[ii] Even wages for grocery store workers grew dramatically—more than 70 percent over the same period.[13] A rising tide *was* lifting all boats.

But something happened in the decades that followed: America's economy continued to grow—but the prosperity wasn't shared. Unfortunately, as we'll see, the headline statistics masked that reality.

---

ii Special trades include plumbing, heating, and air conditioning; painting, paper hanging, and decorating; electrical work; masonry, stonework, and plastering; carpentering and flooring; and roofing and sheet metal work.

Occupation[iii]	1960s salaries in 2023 USD	Today's salaries in 2023 USD
Lawyer	$85,393 (1966)[14]	$145,760 (2023)[15]
Production worker in manufacturing	$54,612 (1966)[16]	$44,960 (2023)[17]
Automobile mechanic	$74,364 (1966)[18]	$47,700 (2023)[19]
CEO at top 350 firms	$847,000 (1965)[20]	$15,968,000 (2023)[21]

DOES A RISING TIDE STILL LIFT ALL BOATS?

Today, many Americans *feel* as though their upward mobility has been curtailed.[22] This raises a fundamental question: Does that feeling comport with the underlying data? In other words, is it possible to measure the degree to which economic prosperity is authentically shared between those nearer the top of the income ladder and those nearer the bottom? Is America already sharing her prosperity sufficiently? Or is the American Dream falling further out of reach for those who might have once believed that hard work and gumption could earn them a better life?

Before delving into the practicalities of measuring shared prosperity, we should acknowledge the statistic that economists and policymakers tend to rely on to gauge overall prosperity is, and remains, gross domestic product, or GDP. Like the GNP previously, GDP is an accepted proxy for prosperity, designed to convey the total income of

---

iii All calculations in this chart were adjusted using the CPI-U found at "Consumer Price Index for All Urban Consumers: All Items in US City Average (CPIAUCSL)," BLS via Federal Reserve Bank of St. Louis, accessed May 23, 2024, https://fred.stlouisfed.org/series /CPIAUCSL.

all people in a given population.[iv] Even tracked across time, however, the figure tells us almost nothing about how that income is distributed *within* the economy.

As illustrated by the next chart, "real GDP" per capita has, in fact, fallen at times—for example, after the dot-com bubble burst in 2001, during the Great Recession in 2008 and 2009, and for a moment in the wake of Covid's initial outbreak in the United States in 2020.[23] But through the broad course of the nation's postwar history, GDP has typically been on the march upward. To that end, someone judging the nation's economy exclusively on the basis of that metric might be led to presume that life has broadly improved over time—that economic prosperity has only been enhanced for everyone. And by some standard, they wouldn't be wrong. But GDP doesn't tell us *how that economic prosperity is distributed*—a distinction that makes a great deal of difference.

The presumption during the postwar era was that the nation was enjoying some modicum of shared prosperity as the economy grew. When the tide was up, everyone's boat was lifted. To this day, many senior political figures continue to embrace that maxim on faith.[24] But the nation as a whole is no longer convinced. As *The Wall Street Journal* reported in late 2023: "Only 36 percent of voters in a new . . .

---

iv There are three ways of calculating GDP, all of which are equal in theory, although empirically they have slight discrepancies: (1) The expenditure approach is the amount spent on consumer expenditures, plus the total investment, plus government spending, plus net exports. (2) The income approach is the total of everyone's income. (3) The value-added approach calculates how, at each step in production, the producer adds some value. For example, when a jeweler buys a diamond and a chain for $1,000 each and then sells a necklace for $3,000, he is adding $3,000–$2,000 = $1,000. Then you add all of these up throughout the economy. "Gross Domestic Product: How It Is Measured," Central Statistics Office (Republic of Ireland), accessed February 10, 2025, https://www.cso.ie/en/interactivezone/statisticsexplained/nationalaccountsexplained/grossdomesticproducthowitismeasured/.

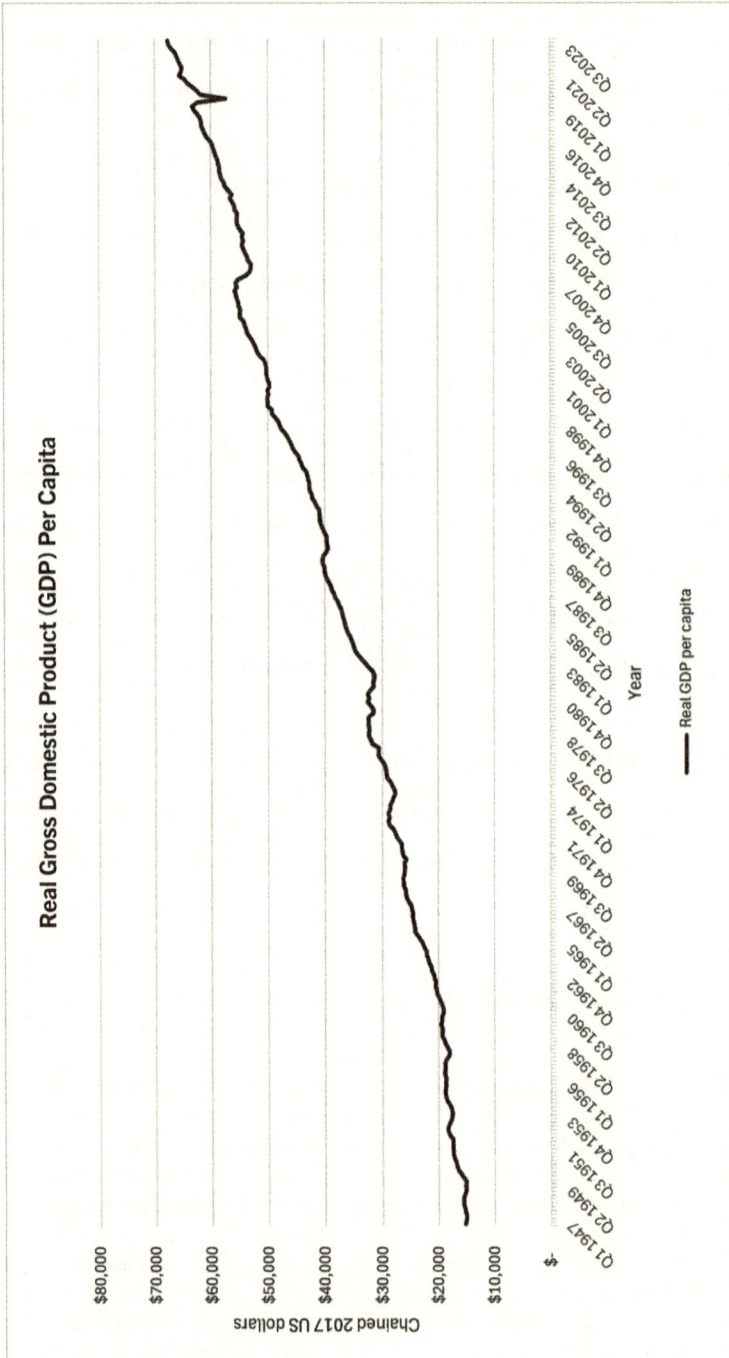

Real Gross Domestic Product (GDP) Per Capita

survey said the American Dream still holds true, substantially fewer than the 53 percent who said so in 2012 and 48 percent in 2016 in similar surveys of adults."[25] And, as we'll see, the reason is clear: Our reliance on GDP has distracted us from the crucial changes in how the nation's prosperity is shared.

Recall the basics: Between 1928 and 1979, the gap between the highest income earners and everyone else actually closed in every state but Alaska. But then, as we noted earlier, the country began to backslide, and the impacts have been profound.[26] In 1963, the wealthiest families had, on average, about six dollars for every single dollar claimed by a family nearer the middle of the pack. By 2013, the ratio had grown to 12:1.[27]

The top-to-bottom income disparity is not, in and of itself, our focus here. Nor are we focused on GDP growth *per se*. Rather, our notion is that shared economic prosperity requires that everyone, rich and poor, benefit meaningfully from economic growth and enhanced *national* prosperity. Everyone who works hard, follows the rules, and strives to achieve should have the opportunity to contribute and prosper, regardless of where they fall on the income ladder. To date, economists and policymakers have yet to set a clear way to measure whether we're making progress in reaching this goal, or even if we're on the right track. Ultimately, the question we need to answer is: Does a rising tide still lift all boats to any meaningful degree?

Set the statistics aside and you quickly discover that Americans are skeptical: In 1999, a full plurality did not perceive life in the United States to be better than it was in the 1950s, with three in ten claiming that life had gotten worse. Perhaps as expected, the poorer the family, the more likely it was for prosperity to appear out of reach.[28] A survey taken during the economic boom at the end of 2023 found that more than half of earners making yearly incomes between $30,000 and $130,000 had a negative view of their finances.[29]

All of which is to say, the picture painted by GDP differs drastically from popular perception. For decades, growth was shared meaningfully by Americans at most, if not all, income levels. But that's not true anymore. From 2001 to 2023, the income growth of the top 1 percent of earners—a whopping 57 percent—outpaced that of any other income quintile, even after accounting for taxes and transfers.[v] In other words, the top 1 percent saw a boost that was twelve times the size of the miserly 5 percent growth seen by the middle 60 percent of earners, and roughly seven times more than the income growth experienced by the bottom 60 percent of earners.[30]

What we need, separate from GDP, is a measure that provides us with a more fulsome sense of economic growth-sharing. Such a metric can inspire and empower policies that ensure growth does not leave a significant segment of the population behind. And that is what LISEP researchers have sought to create.

CRAFTING A MEASURE OF SHARED ECONOMIC PROSPERITY

To paint a more realistic picture of economic well-being, we first need an objective measure of what might be considered the *opportunity* for citizens

---

v We focus on disposable income, which is defined as total income after taxes and inclusive of all cash government transfer payments, such as Social Security benefits, welfare benefits, and food stamps. It excludes in-kind transfers, such as Medicare and Medicaid, which provide nonmonetary benefits.

to climb past their parents. That's not to suggest that every successive generation in every individual family necessarily needs to make more than the last: The son of a Fortune 500 CEO may choose to become a teacher. A lawyer's daughter might choose to become the manager of a small shop on Main Street. But in order to maintain the *potential* of upward mobility, a family objectively needs to make more than what's required to cover their True Living Cost, as outlined in the previous chapter.

To determine the minimum amount of income required to obtain the American Dream, LISEP has crafted a new metric: the Minimal Quality of Life index, or MQL. The MQL was not an easy statistic to compile, because individual households maintain different spending habits. Nonetheless, there is a discernible standard of living—perhaps better described as a certain standard of economic freedom—that is a prerequisite to climbing the economic ladder. A family needs income sufficient to afford childcare in the early years, to send their children to quality public schools, and to cover the costs of attending a local trade school or university.[vi] They need the financial wherewithal to eat out or order in when busy schedules don't permit them to cook.[31] To gather with family and friends for special holiday celebrations. To take even a short annual trip and a few weekend outings. They need the freedom, for example, to attend a movie once every couple of months. To subscribe to a basic suite of streaming services (generally far cheaper today than cable). To purchase the pair of sneakers or tennis racquet required to maintain a healthy exercise regimen.[32]

---

vi The MQL considers the minimal amount of savings a family would need, on average, to send their child to a public university to pursue a four-year bachelor's degree, presuming they pay in-state tuition and receive financial aid. Alternatively, these savings should be able to cover other educational paths out of high school that a student might desire, such as a trade school.

These costs rise above subsistence, of course—but they're hardly extravagant. Some may quibble with the details of our model, which is set out below. But after a series of robustness checks, we've concluded that this cost burden represents the prerequisite for achieving the American Dream. If a household *can't* cover this suite of bills, it's much more difficult to get ahead.

Our challenge is not simply to track how the MQL has evolved. We can't simply measure how the collective burden of covering that suite of expenses has changed through the decades. We also need to understand how the MQL interacts with the nation's income growth as a whole. Has the overall growth, as depicted by the GDP, expanded the universe of Americans living above the MQL? Has the percentage of the population living above the MQL threshold stayed the same? Or, as opinion surveys seems to suggest, are more Americans perversely finding it more difficult to achieve a minimum quality of life?

Here, we really need to be cognizant of the GDP data and why it distorts our impression of reality. Between 2001 and 2023, American GDP rose by 57.2 percent, and GDP *per capita* grew by 33.8 percent.[33] Nevertheless, there was little change in the average income of Americans in the bottom 60 percent.[34] Real incomes for those in the bottom three quintiles rose a mere 8.5 percent in that period, or an average of 0.4 percent per year.[vii] Consider that fact: For nearly a quarter century, the prevailing indicator of prosperity has suggested that the American economy is growing at a remarkable pace—yet 60 percent of the country has experienced almost no discernible improvement.

---

vii This population does not include Americans over the age of sixty-five throughout the time period, as it is usual for Americans to retire at or after this age, which lowers their incomes. If we would have included them in the sample, it might have falsely conveyed the slowdown of income growth when really that slowdown was just a demographic shift. Including them in this sample lowers the 8.5 percent number to 6.9 percent.

WHAT IS INCLUDED IN THE MINIMAL QUALITY OF LIFE METRIC?

Housing: Adequate housing must ensure secure tenure, offer functional water and utilities, guarantee safety, and meet the family's needs. It must be located a reasonable distance from work and community resources. The MQL allocates the cost of shelter plus utilities in a decent unit as well as basic costs for furniture, appliances, and other household products that make the unit habitable and comfortable.

Health care: The MQL includes premiums and out-of-pocket fees for employer-provided health insurance. Personal care expenses such as laundry, clothing storage, and hygiene/cosmetics products are included as they're key to maintaining daily cleanliness and physical well-being.

Food: In addition to nutritionally adequate groceries, the MQL includes occasional meals away from the home, recognizing the substantial investment of time required to consistently prepare meals at home. The MQL also tracks the cost of hosting five guests for a singular celebratory meal (e.g., a holiday gathering) during the year.

Transportation: Budgeting for transportation covers daily commuting and modest annual travel. The MQL accounts for the expenses of a used car, insurance, maintenance, fuel for fifteen thousand miles of everyday commuting and travel-related driving, and additional travel costs such as meals and lodging.

Raising a family: The cost of raising a family is determined by a parent's ability to create a platform that provides children an opportunity to pursue the American Dream. These costs are described below.

Childcare. The MQL includes adequate childcare costs (as does the TLC), accounting for year-round care for four-year-olds and seasonal care for school-aged children.

(continued)

Education. The MQL ensures families can save adequately to afford a four-year college degree at a public, in-state university for their children—with a typical financial-aid package but without loans—improving their children's chances for good pay, adequate career choices, and intergenerational mobility.

Toys. The MQL incorporates a toy budget for households with children. This budget is not tied to the price of specific toys but rather reflects the amount a middle-income family, assumed to be budget-conscious, would likely spend on toys per child annually.

Youth sports. The MQL covers the expenses of sports gear for a child playing one of the top five high school sports, so families can support their kids' physical activity and development of social and competitive skills. However, the MQL does not track the cost of sports participation fees for public school sports due to a lack of consistently published data available.

Technology: Technology costs ensure households are digitally connected for work, education, and other activities basic to life in the twenty-first century. Building on the TLC, which tracks the cost of smartphones, a household computer, and internet and phone service, the MQL includes the cost of a TV.

Clothing: The MQL expands the TLC's coverage of clothing costs to include essential fitness gear for adults. It accounts for an annual pair of new athletic shoes.

Basic leisure: The MQL includes a budget for common free-time activities. It covers costs associated with watching TV, factoring in both streaming services and conventional satellite or cable. Moreover, the MQL accounts for outings by budgeting for each person to attend six movies and two MLB games each year.

Don't misinterpret that to mean the circumstances have been uniform among middle- and low-income earners. Households in the middle quintile—those earning roughly $50,100 annually with one income or $87,900 with two—typically have enough to cover the basics that constitute the TLC, as discussed earlier in the book. On average, however, they still sit $11,600 short of the MQL. And as we've seen, many have wallowed there for more than two decades, even as GDP has grown so dramatically.

Not unexpectedly, the story is significantly more dire for those in the two lowest quintiles. The single-earner household sitting between the twentieth and fortieth percentiles makes a yearly average of $31,800 after taxes, while dual-income households make $56,000 on average. As a result, the average household in this bracket fails by $33,800 to attain enough to meet the MQL; furthermore, they remain $22,100 short of their subsistence TLC.

Households in the lowest quintile—those who make, on average, a mere $10,700 yearly with a single earner in the home or $21,700 with two earners in the home—are a full $34,100 below their TLC, meaning that their income gets them slightly less than a quarter of the MQL.

Income Range	Average income for single-headed households (2023)[viii]	Average income for dual-headed households (2023)	Average amount *below* the MQL (2023)
Bottom 60 percent	$28,800	$65,600	$29,200
0–20 percent	$10,700	$21,700	$42,100
20–40 percent	$31,800	$56,000	$33,800
40–60 percent	$50,100	$87,900	$11,600

viii Estimates in this table are rounded to the nearest hundred dollars.

Yet the most remarkable element binding these households together is not their shared inability to attain the American Dream. It's that their frustrating predicament has remained relatively stable over the past quarter-century *even as the nation's GDP rose.* Earners in the top two quintiles saw their incomes grow about three times faster than those in the bottom 60 percent.[35] In 2023, the top 40 percent exceeded the MQL, on average, by more than $127,000. This means that while the bottom 60 percent were bonded together in stagnation, the top 40 percent were pulling away.

Income Range	Average income for single-headed households (2023)[ix]	Average income for dual-headed households (2023)	Average amount *above* the MQL (2023)
Top 40 percent	$114,200	$276,800	$127,800
60–80 percent	$71,800	$136,600	$27,100
80–100 percent	$173,500	$381,700	$228,500

The MQL renders a view of the economic landscape that reveals, in stark contrast, why so many American workers remain frustrated with the nation's economy: They've been unable to get ahead even during boom times. As those nearer the top of the income scale have thrived, their fellow citizens have been left to endure the indignity of making difficult trade-offs: whether to forgo a car repair or skip a trip to the doctor, whether to take a second job or spend more time with a troubled child. These are not just hypotheticals; people are making these types of sacrifices en masse. And over the years, the constant feeling of swimming against the current has taken a collective toll.

---

ix   Estimates in this table are rounded to the nearest hundred dollars.

In 2021, more than fifty-three million people "turned to food banks, food pantries and meal programs for help"—30 percent more than two years prior.[36] In 2022, 35 percent of adults reported putting off medical care for themselves or a family member as a result of unaffordability.[37] Even though homeless shelters have added more beds in recent years, the number of unsheltered homeless individuals has risen 35 percent since 2015.[38] And while only 29 percent of adults aged eighteen to twenty-nine lived with their parents in 1960, this number reached 38 percent by 2000, hit 47 percent in 2019, and peaked at over 52 percent during the Covid-19 pandemic.[39] Clearly, these frustrations aren't born of mere "vibes"—they reflect reality. The hours that working- and middle-class Americans work merely to tread water have risen, simply because their average hourly income has fallen in real terms.

Between 1980 and 2022, the median hourly income for households with adults in their thirties fell from nearly $23.61 to $23.07 (in constant 2022 dollars, adjusted using the CPI-U).[x] Households headed by thirty-something adults at the thirtieth percentile saw median wages fall from $16.99 to $16.82. Meanwhile, comparable households in the top 25 percent saw their hourly income grow from $40.64 to $47.12, and households in the top 10 percent saw a jump from $51.23 to $67.31.[40]

And that's the essence of the problem—the reason why so many Americans feel as though they're slipping down the ladder of prosperity: They have less to show for their hours of extra toil. For many,

---

x As suggested in chapter 3, however, the CPI-U understates cost-of-living changes for the lower- and middle-income population, so the figures in this paragraph are likely underestimating the true value of 1980s earnings.

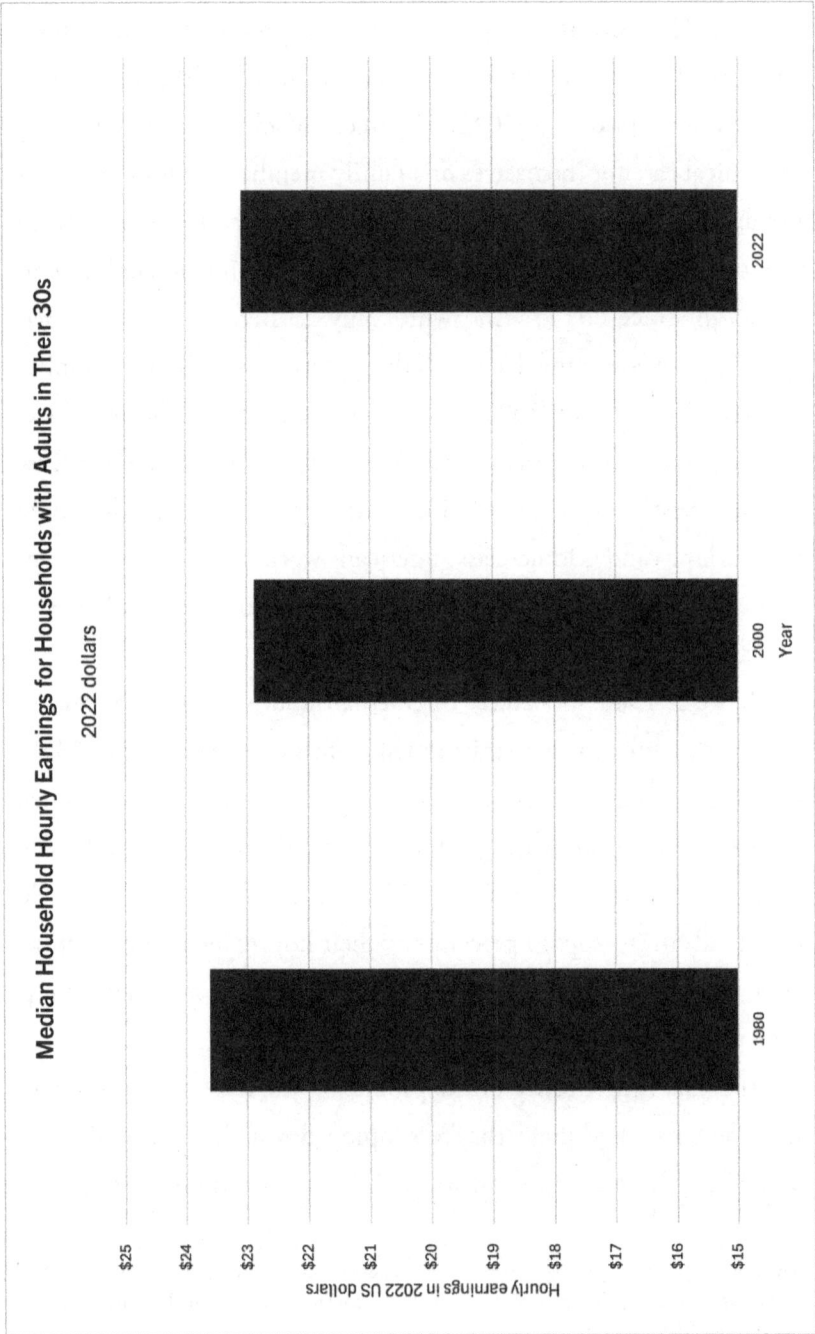

Median Household Hourly Earnings for Households with Adults in Their 30s

2022 dollars

these circumstances invariably feel like a vicious carnival game—one in which the odds are stacked against them and the house almost always wins. But even as they bristle, they know there's no way out. If they stop playing, they're sure to lose—and if they fail to keep pace, they're sure to fall back.

THE IMPACTS OF HOARDED GROWTH

In sum, a rising tide does *not* lift all boats anymore—it lifts too few boats. But this fundamental shift, born largely from the amalgam of effects described in the previous three chapters—high functional unemployment, lower real wages, more profound inflation, static real incomes—is too often missed or ignored in Washington. As a result, those who shape US economic policy have been misled by the headline statistics into misunderstanding reality on the ground.

Across the country, many have experienced this change viscerally; they know from everyday experience that the prevailing statistics don't line up with reality. And those who have feet in both worlds—those who have witnessed the degree to which working-class life has gotten worse even as GDP has grown—are therefore even more incredulous. The American Dream, they note, isn't out of reach because the nation has collectively become poorer—in fact, they argue the country is more prosperous. But the bottom 60 percent of households have seen their yearly income grow by a mere $3,000 over the past twenty-three years, while the top 5 percent saw an increase of $157,800 (in 2023 dollars).

Is it any wonder that America remains cynical even during periods of rapid overall growth? At the current rate, it would take roughly 1,163 years for the bottom 60 percent to match the dollar improvement that the top 5 percent enjoyed in little more than two decades. That disparity has arisen not simply from the fact that certain jobs have seen wages rise more rapidly than others. Rather, many of the jobs that once served as rungs up the ladder of prosperity have either disappeared or been reduced to providing a pittance of their former wages.

Between 1976 and 2023, the nation's manufacturing sector (which often paid a decent salary) fell from 17.5 million jobs to 12.9 million, while the retail and leisure and hospitality sectors (which tend to pay less) grew from 9 million jobs to 15.5 million, and from 5.8 million jobs to 16.6 million, respectively.[41] So, even if you set aside the impact that higher-paying jobs requiring advanced degrees have in differentiating wage statistics, the positions now available to the working class are, on average, also less remunerative in real terms.

Moreover, gains have diverged *within* many professions; that is, certain professions have seen incomes rise substantially for only a subset of workers. LISEP investigated individuals' total annual income from wages or self-employment income in several professions that historically represent productive and fairly stable employment, across a variety of levels of education attainment and required professional experience. Financial managers earning incomes at the fortieth percentile across their profession, for example, saw their wages grow by 6.4 percent between 1976 and 2022—while those in the higher-earning eightieth percentile, by contrast, enjoyed a 35.6 percent raise. Editors, news analysts, reporters, and media correspondents at the eightieth percentile saw a modest 7.6 percent increase in real wages—but their counterparts at the fortieth percentile experienced

a real-wage decline of 7.5 percent. Among automotive service technicians and mechanics at the eightieth percentile, real wages fell
12.7 percent; among those at the fortieth percentile, the decline was a
whopping 27.2 percent.[42]

This divergence in wages is, of course, not the only takeaway from
wage distributions of the selected occupations; some occupations that
pay close to the minimum wage saw lower percentiles rising faster or
falling slower than higher percentiles, and some followed their own
trends. However, the notable wage divergence within these occupations illustrates that even within traditionally stable career paths, the
ability to share in economic prosperity varies dramatically.

But the focus on how much people make vis-à-vis other people
can distract from the more salient point: No matter how robust economic growth is, Americans living below a certain threshold too often
toil on a treadmill to nowhere.[43] In 2018, the average middle-class,
married couple worked six hundred more hours per year than in 1975;
despite that extra effort, many remained downwardly mobile.[44] It is
one thing to accept that you're making a small fraction of the CEO's
salary but entirely another to realize you're sinking despite expend-
ing more effort than those who worked similar jobs decades earlier.
Low-income workers—those in the bottom quintile of earners—have
seen their incomes rise a mere 12 percent since 2001, and that miserly
growth means they're still, on average, more than $42,100 short of
the American Dream.[xi] As one Brown University economist put it, the
present reality "feeds a growing sense of economic ennui."[45]

---

xi The average income of the bottom quintile in 2001 was $10,749.10 (in 2023 dollars). In 2023,
    it was $12,035.57—a mere 12 percent rise.

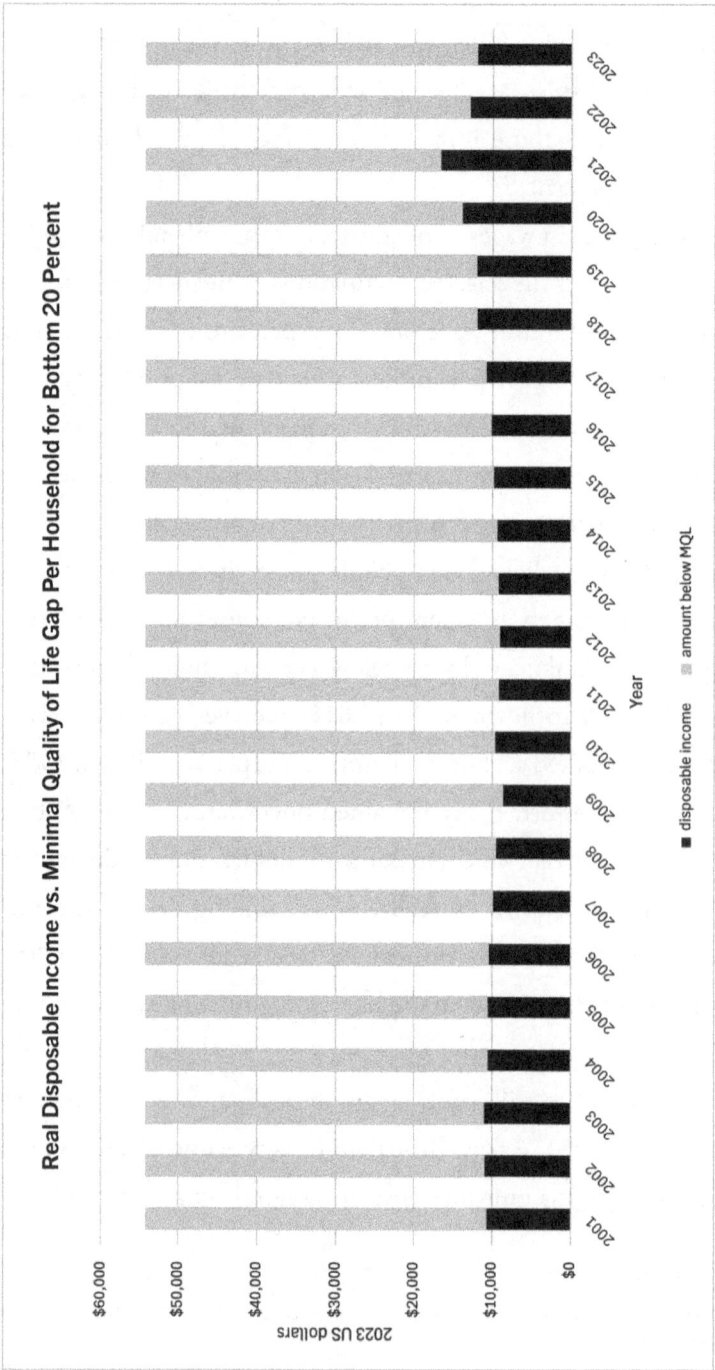

Real Disposable Income vs. Minimal Quality of Life Gap Per Household for Bottom 20 Percent

The impacts are pervasive and exacerbated in large part because, as detailed in the previous chapter, inflation has proven to be so profound. The median home cost a little more than $100,000 in 1960 (in 2020 dollars); in 2019, by contrast, accounting for inflation, the cost was more than $240,000. That's a price increase of 129 percent in real terms—more than double—even as the median household income has risen only 39 percent.[46] It should, of course, come as no surprise that more than 80 percent of those in the top quintile of earners own their homes, while fewer than half of those in the bottom quintile can boast the same.[47] We suspect that with the increase in mortgage rates that has occurred during the past couple of years, these figures will be even more dispiriting in the years to come.

But it's not just housing. The amount families must spend to send their children to a public, four-year, in-state university has more than doubled since 2001. Travel expenses have grown 170 percent, and the cost of eating out has increased 134 percent. And while TV subscriptions and basic sports equipment can be acquired for less than in 2001, these savings distract from the broader narrative.[48] A poll in 2022 found that more than one in three Americans were delaying medical care for themselves or a family member on account of their ability, or inability, to pay for it.[49]

For most, the American Dream seems further away than ever.

A MORE COMPLETE MEASURE OF SHARED PROSPERITY

But knowing broadly that the American Dream has become more elusive for large swaths of the population isn't enough. To glean a clearer picture over time, we need an indicator that reaches beyond the limitations of GDP and inequality. And that requires a way to simultaneously track two separate elements: prosperity and sharing. This task begins with selecting the right data—namely, total disposable income, a statistic defined as the money all households in the United States have to spend, save, or invest after taxes and transfers.[xii] We need, in short, a way to not only understand the total amount of disposable income available to Americans but also whether that income is being distributed in a way that ensures all households have the opportunity to achieve a minimal quality of life. In other words, is economic growth truly being shared equitably among the hardworking Americans who contribute to it?

That then leads to a simple question: To reach true *shared* prosperity, how much sharing would be required? Put differently, if we wanted to ensure everyone had a chance to claim the American Dream, how much *more* of the nation's aggregate disposable income would need to flow to those with insufficient income to meet the MQL?

To answer this question, LISEP disaggregated the American population into two groups: The top 40 percent of earners (the top two quintiles) typically have disposable income above the MQL. By contrast, many within the bottom 60 percent (the bottom three quintiles) have disposable income that falls below the MQL. At issue is how much more of America's disposable income would need to be allotted to the bottom 60 percent such that they collectively have enough to

---

xii While "disposable income" might seem like it refers to money left over after necessities are purchased, in economic terms, it specifically excludes those expenses. When referring to spendable income that remains after taxes, transfers, and necessities are purchased, "discretionary income" is the preferred term. Here, we've adopted the technical definition of the term "disposable income."

begin climbing the ladder of prosperity. So, LISEP researchers crafted the Shared Economic Prosperity measure (SEP), which hinges on the relationship between these two discrete figures.

First, the statistic determines the *target share* at any given moment—namely, the estimated percentage of total disposable income that the bottom 60 percent would need to reach the MQL.[xiii] Second, the SEP incorporates the *actual share*—namely, the percentage of disposable income currently going to the bottom 60 percent. By understanding where each of the two measures land at any given moment, the SEP tracks whether the economy is sharing more or less of its prosperity.

Take, as an example, 2023. That year, the bottom 60 percent of earners would have needed 39 percent of the nation's earnings to lift every individual to the MQL—that, then, was the *target* share. But the bottom 60 percent *actually* claimed only 22.1 percent, leaving a vast gap. That gap could have been closed by either of two economic mechanisms or by a combination of both: Greater prosperity (more aggregate disposable income) would have brought the *target* share down. More sharing (more disposable income going to the bottom three quintiles) would have brought the *actual* share up. The key to understanding the SEP is to look at each figure in relation to the other and then to analyze the shifts over time.

Consider a few additional illustrations. Between 2001 and 2002, the *target* share fell from 42.8 percent to 42 percent—a shift

---

xiii Note that as the country's disposable income rises, the target falls because a smaller share of the aggregate would provide a sufficient sum to ensure everyone had a shot at the American Dream. If the total disposable income does not rise, in nominal terms, faster than the MQL for the bottom 60 percent, the cost of achieving the basic American Dream will be further out of reach for that group after adjusting for cost of living.

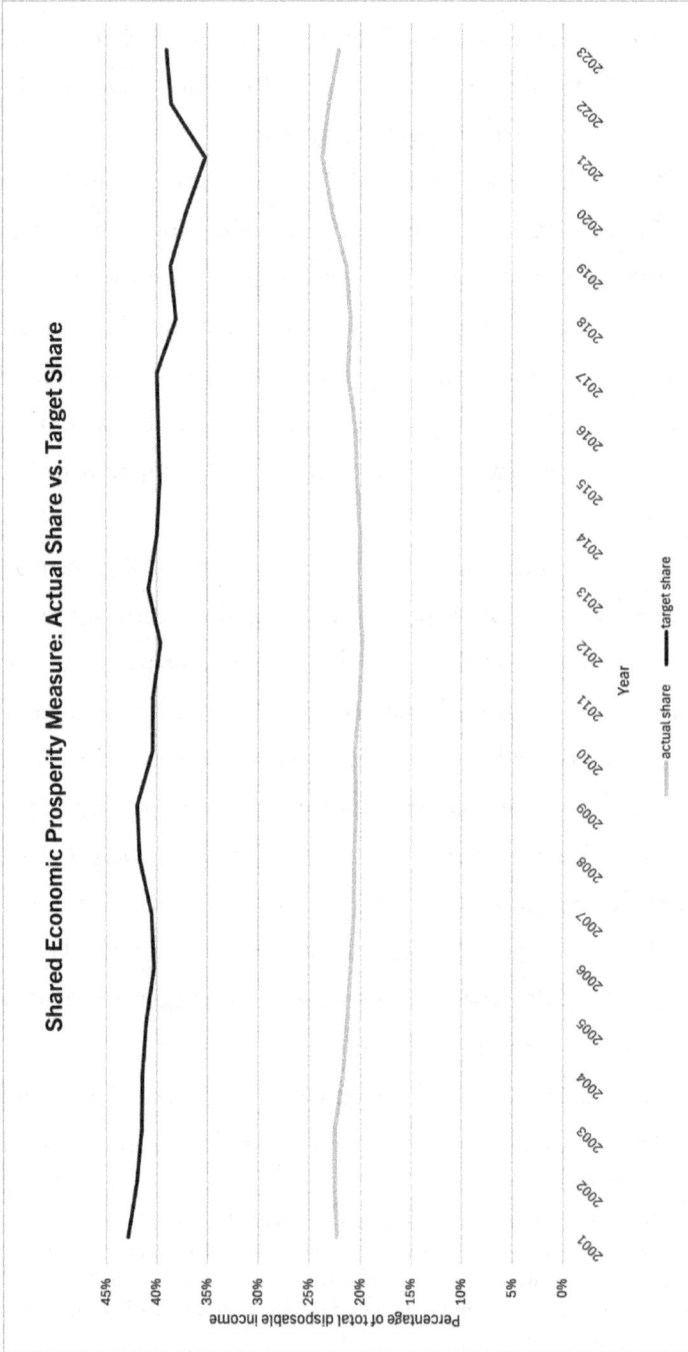

Shared Economic Prosperity Measure: Actual Share vs. Target Share

revealing that the economy was growing such that those in the bottom three quintiles could have reached the MQL with a smaller slice of the nation's disposable income. As it was, their *actual* share of that income grew on the margins at the very same time, from 22.3 percent to 22.5 percent. In short, in the wake of the economic expansion that occurred during the Clinton era, the nation was getting wealthier *and* low- and middle-income Americans were enjoying a slightly larger slice of the nation's disposable income. Between 2003 and 2004, however, something else happened: The target decreased marginally, from 41.5 percent to 41.4 percent, because the cost of meeting the MQL for the bottom 60 percent rose at nearly the same pace as total disposable income did. But the actual share fell from 22.5 percent to 21.7 percent. In short, those in the lower three quintiles fell further behind.

The economy evolved in different ways between 2017 and 2018: It was still growing, meaning that the lower three quintiles needed a smaller share of the nation's disposable income to meet the MQL—in fact, the target fell from 40 percent to 38.1 percent. But despite the nation's broader prosperity, the bottom three quintiles saw their slice of the nation's disposable income fall from 21.2 percent to 21 percent. By contrast, as disposable income shrank between 2021 and 2022—during the pandemic—the target for the bottom three quintiles grew from 35.2 percent to 38.5 percent.[xiv] Yet their actual share fell during that time, from 23.7 percent to 23.1 percent, marking a trend that would continue into 2023. In short, the nation's low- and

---

xiv This was a result of the fact that the bottom 60 percent was either no longer receiving pandemic assistance or saw a reduction in assistance, while the top quintiles largely saw passive income losses as asset values deflated.

moderate-income households needed more to achieve the MQL, but they were getting less.

Crucially, the SEP illustrates why the target shares and actual shares, while noteworthy in and of themselves, really need to be interpreted in tandem. When trying to gauge whether sharing has improved or fallen off, it may be tempting simply to note the gap between the two, but the most revealing picture can be gleaned only by looking at both the target and actual figures *together*. And, here, the reason for the nation's continuing frustration—what the professor at Brown termed "ennui"—comes into clear perspective: Since 2001, as total disposable income has grown by 24.9 percent, the target share has fallen from 42.8 percent to 39 percent. In other words, because the economy was growing, those in the bottom 60 percent needed a smaller share of the nation's prosperity to meet MQL. Yet progress toward closing this gap has been slow—their *actual* share fell from 22.3 percent to 22.1 percent. Instead of working to increase the actual share received by the bottom 60 percent, our nation has relied on overall economic growth outpacing MQL. At the current rate of progress, it will take more than two centuries to achieve true shared prosperity.

This is perhaps the most instructive element of LISEP's broader exploration of the nation's prevailing economic statistics. Over the course of nearly a quarter century, as the American economy was enjoying profound prosperity, people in the working class and middle class made almost no progress toward creating a real foundation for achieving the American Dream. Yet because growth was so robust, they *could* have seen their lots improve even as the top two quintiles continued to maintain average incomes well above MQL. Put another way, in 2023, the American economy could have distributed the nation's prosperity such that the bottom 60 percent reached the MQL while those in the top 40 percent retained an average income of $157,622, which translates to $84,024 above the MQL.[50]

Taken together, the bottom line is surprising—but also important and hopeful: America need not accept a devil's bargain between high-end prosperity and economic stagnation. Our economy *absolutely* can share prosperity more broadly, and doing so would benefit *everyone*. We can, in short, have our cake and eat it too.

A growing economy could, in fact, boost everyone above the MQL. America *could,* in fact, meet the SEP's target share. A rising tide could, once again, lift all boats. We could offer middle- and low-income Americans real hope for a brighter future.

And in so doing, we could restore the American Dream.

Conclusion

As the preceding chapters make clear, the headline statistics we currently employ to understand America's economy are profoundly misleading. Too many of us have come to embrace rosier notions of how middle- and low-income Americans fare than reality bears out. Since 2001, unemployment has generally been higher, wages have generally been lower, and inflation has generally been more severe than the prevailing indicators lead us to believe—particularly for middle- and low-income Americans. And the growing chasm separating perception and reality, we at LISEP believe, is largely responsible for the widespread frustration that America is on the wrong track, even when the economy is purportedly booming.[1] Until Americans, at long last, begin to see the nation's travails through a lens that is much closer to the truth, we are too likely to remain lost and on the verge of a social explosion.

Changing course demands we embrace a three-pronged strategy.

1. Change the Statistics We Employ to Understand the Economy

First, and perhaps most obvious, we need to change the statistics we employ to understand the economy. That was made clear in the first three chapters of this book. Without a clear target, how can even well-meaning policymakers formulate and execute effective policy? In addition, the substance of chapter 4 demands particular attention. Here, not only does the GDP figure mask some of the nuances of US growth, but its presentation frequently suggests a shared prosperity that is far from the truth.

It's not just that we've failed to grasp what's *really* happening with unemployment, earnings, and prices—it's that, on balance, it seems that GDP has actually grown quite decently even as the nation's middle and working classes struggled ever more mightily to tread water. The top 1 percent—and even more so, the top 0.1 percent—have become avatars for the European nobles who once lived a world apart from those struggling nearby. Taken together, this economic reality of twenty-first-century America—sliding incomes for middle- and low-income Americans amid rapidly expanding wealth at the top— is ominous. Why? Because economic growth has not been robustly shared, if shared at all. Our concern also stems from a worry that the decline in the well-being of middle- and lower-income Americans may be contributing to the rise of severe social and political complications.

On this front, though, we need to guard against confusing *correlation* with *causation*. That said, the economic metamorphosis of the past quarter-century has undoubtedly coincided with a range of other worrying trends, some of which have already become clear. The handwriting is on the wall: Suicide rates are up, and life expectancy is down.[2] Academic test scores have fallen.[3] Drug overdoses overwhelm big and small communities alike.[4] Homeless tent cities remain a reality of most American cities, while private aircraft usage edges toward record highs.[5] And while no one institution can be held single-handedly responsible for the present state of affairs, too many of those who traverse the corridors of power have, too often, chosen to be overly measured in their responses to these economic and social problems. Programmatic changes, they worry, come with steep costs, including slowing GDP growth. Others are willing to drive change but remain blind to the real impact of the changes they champion—obscured by rosy government statistics that mask who wins and who loses from policy choices.

Our concern here is that the impulse not to rock the boat, or to rock it the wrong way, has been born of an epidemic blindness to the reality: The boat has already begun to list. Beyond any concern about the social disruption that could arise from a more aggressive economic policy, we need to be on guard for the potential for political violence.

No society will ever be able to easily metabolize the civil unrest that comes from widespread downward mobility. But the attendant problems in a nation that prides itself on an ever-upward trajectory for all who work hard and play by the rules—namely, the American Dream—are proving particularly stark. Yet because we depend on a bevy of statistics that mask the truth, too many economic experts, political leaders, and policymakers simply aren't cognizant of the serious situation facing those elsewhere in the country.

The trouble is not restricted to the statistical masking of the economic realities. Societal divisions—gated communities, exclusive clubs, luxury resorts—create a physical and emotional distance that hinders the elite's ability to fully grasp the realities faced by lower-income demographics. The digital "filter bubbles" that blind communities to the plights of those who live nearby have served much the same end. Consider again the French Revolution, which did not emerge exclusively from rampant inequality but because the political elite neglected to grapple honestly with how bad things had gotten for the main population. They either refused to fully understand or were unable—intellectually or emotionally—to confront reality. Perhaps for some an analogy to the French Revolution seems too extreme—no one on the American political landscape is explicitly saying anything quite so preposterous as "let them eat cake." But neither have we seen Washington react with the urgency, vigor, or focused understanding that the moment—and the lived reality of our fellow citizens—demands.

Few are calling for a new GDP sharing ratio—and those who do often lack the rigor we argue is essential in the final chapter. That chapter also makes a perhaps surprising case: We can achieve a more equitable and sustainable distribution without impoverishing any group, including the top 0.1 percent. This brings us to the second crucial point.

2. Measure As Accurately As We Can the True Efficacy of Policy Proposals

Our failure to craft an accurate statistical composite of the nation's economic reality makes it much harder to shape highly effective policy responses. It's like we're firing artillery at an enemy battleship without any way of knowing if the shells are on target.

Plausible pathways out of America's current economic swamp

have been suggested by many thought leaders. A number of these prospects are enumerated in my first book, *The Vanishing American Dream*. We can—and should—expand access to education, change our tax system, make our health care system more proficient and efficient, help American businesses expand and hire additional workers, and augment opportunity zones. But we also need to adopt more rigorous statistical mechanisms for evaluating the genuine impact of each proposed intervention. What "bang for the buck" are we really getting from the program, however well-meaning and facially appealing it might appear?

Under the current statistical regime, we're liable to misinterpret the results. Does Program A *really* reduce unemployment? Using today's prevailing measure, a company could vastly expand its roster of poverty-wage jobs, and it might *appear* that we were making progress—but when using the True Rate of Unemployment, the truth would come out. Does Program B effectively raise earnings? Today's prevailing measure might not detect the impact of a deluge of poorly paid part-time positions, whereas the True Weekly Earnings would be much more likely to accurately inform those evaluating the program.

Replacing the Consumer Price Index with the True Living Cost index, let alone the Minimal Quality of Life index, would immediately impact the quality of life for those who are dependent on pensions, Social Security checks, and minimum wages, by ensuring that their respective draws kept up more effectively with the cost of maintaining their standard expenses. But getting *all* the numbers right could have much more widespread and positive long-term impacts. The broader question is, how can better metrics provide us with a more comprehensive understanding of which policy interventions work well and which should be discontinued?

And that, then, brings us to the third prong of our call to action.

3. Continue Refining the Statistics We Use to Measure the Nation's Economy

As we've seen, old methodologies fail to account for broad changes in the nation's economic reality. And so, to much the same degree that GDP is an inappropriate measure of general prosperity, we want to ensure that our new proposed measure of Shared Economic Prosperity—the SEP—is further refined to give those making important economic decisions a clear picture of how those in the middle class and the working class are faring. We don't want to fall into the same trap of publishing statistics that are less accurate than they could be—or risk letting them become misleading in the decades ahead as society evolves and demands better metrics.

To that end, we at LISEP intend to foment discussions in the months and years to come about what the MQL should be, refining the metric as necessary. We hope others join in that work, allowing us to further refine the SEP and delineate more specifically what additional economic sharing ratios produce what results. Happily, we believe American economic growth can be sufficiently robust to bring everyone to par *without* requiring the kind of redistribution that can upend societies. But only further examination and analysis can prove our supposition.

Furthermore, we plan to periodically refine our statistics to ensure they continue to reflect lived reality as accurately as possible—and we hope others, including the government, will do the same.

CR

Finally, I cannot praise highly enough the excellent research team behind this work and the wonderful communications team that helped develop this book. But LISEP alone will not be able to accomplish these three critical missions. The challenge of refashioning the lens we all use to interpret economic reality demands collective concern. The good news is, however, that once the picture is brought into proper focus, we're almost sure to find that the core values that have long shaped America's upward trajectory remain intact. Our research for both this book and *The Vanishing American Dream* has reinforced our faith that the vast majority of Americans want a hand up, not a handout—that working-age adults want to earn a living wage through their own toil. Accordingly, we expect that a clearer picture will spur society-wide efforts to create living-wage jobs. To that end, comparative analyses of metropolitan efforts to enhance *shared* prosperity will help identify the very best ways to serve middle- and low-income American households.

That's why we ask everyone who understands the role misleading statistics play in hampering America's quest for shared prosperity to join our cause. The headline statistics need to be revised as suggested in the previous pages. Our alternative indexes need to be preeminent—or at least published prominently alongside the current set of headline statistics. Too many of the problems we face in America today are tied up in our continuing blindness to the lived experiences of our vast middle- and low-income populations. We urge you to join us in advocating for reforms that bring the truth to light.

Notes

Introduction

1   Eugene Nelson White, "The French Revolution and the Politics of Government Finance, 1770–1815," Journal of Economic History 55, no. 2 (1995): 227–55, http ://www.jstor.org/stable/2123552 (pp. 229–34 are particularly relevant); *Britannica*, "King and Parlements," last updated February 6, 2025, https://www.britannica.com /place/France/King-and-parlements.

2   Mike Duncan, "Climate Chaos Helped Spark the French Revolution—and Holds a Dire Warning for Today," *TIME*, October 20, 2021, https://time.com/6107671/french -revolution-history-climate/; *Britannica*, "Did Marie-Antoinette Really Say 'Let Them Eat Cake'?," accessed February 6, 2025, https://www.britannica.com/story/did-marie -antoinette-really-say-let-them-eat-cake.

3   S. Mintz and S. McNeil, "1930s: Why It Happened," Digital History, 2018, accessed February 6, 2025, https://www.digitalhistory.uh.edu/disp_textbook_print.cfm?smtid =2&psid=3432.

4   Kimberly Amadeo, "1920s Economy," *The Balance*, last updated May 24, 2024, https ://www.thebalancemoney.com/roaring-twenties-4060511.

5   Mark Thornton, "Who Predicted the Great Depression?," chap. 13 in *The Skyscraper Curse: And How Austrian Economists Predicted Every Major Economic Crisis of the Last Century* (Mises Institute, 2018), https://mises.org/online-book/skyscraper-curse-and -how-austrian-economists-predicted-every-major-economic-crisis-last-century/chapter -13-who-predicted-great-depression#footnote17_gxKUhAMyE6Fc.

6   "Stock Market Crash of 1929," Federal Reserve History, accessed February 6, 2025, https://www.federalreservehistory.org/essays/stock-market-crash-of-1929.

7   Melvin I. Urofsky, "Depression," chap. 27 in *Louis D. Brandeis: A Life* (Schocken Books, 2009).

8   Urofsky, "Democracy in the Workplace," chap. 10., *Louis D. Brandeis;* Urofsky, "Depression."

9   "Concepts and Definitions (CPS): Employed," US Bureau of Labor Statistics, accessed February 6, 2025, https://www.bls.gov/cps/definitions.htm#employed.

10   S. Mintz and S. McNeil, "1930s: Why It Happened."

11   Mintz and McNeil, "The Farmers' Plight," Digital History, 2018, accessed February 6, 2025, https://www.digitalhistory.uh.edu/disp_textbook.cfm?smtid=2&psid=3441.

12   Mintz and McNeil, "1930s: Why It Happened."

13   The average difference between the True Rate of Unemployment (TRU) and the BLS headline unemployment indicator (known as "the U-3") over the time period we have studied is 23.4 percentage points. This number is not always constant, though, and the gap has shrunk in recent years, signaling that more of the U-3 jobs also qualify as functional employment as defined by the TRU. "True Rate of Unemployment," Ludwig Institute for Shared Economic Prosperity, accessed April 18, 2024, https://www.lisep .org/tru; "How the Government Measures Unemployment: Who Is Counted as Employed?" US Bureau of Labor Statistics, accessed February 6, 2025, https://www.bls .gov/cps/cps_htgm.htm#employed.

14   The widely used headline statistic derived from the Current Population Survey (CPS)— median weekly earnings of full-time wage and salary workers—is published in a quarterly report, e.g., "Usual Weekly Earnings of Wage and Salary Workers: Fourth Quarter 2024," US Bureau of Labor Statistics, January 22, 2025, https://www.bls.gov/news.release/pdf /wkyeng.pdf; although the BLS also publishes other earnings metrics, none are as comprehensive or widely used as this one. (More information about the relevant terms can be found at "Concepts and Definitions (CPS)," US Bureau of Labor Statistics, accessed February 6, 2025, https://www.bls.gov/cps/definitions.htm#earningswagesalary.) The same earnings report also publishes a separate, less widely used statistic for part-time wage and salaried workers, but this indicator also falls short by excluding most members of the workforce. The Current Employment Statistics (CES) survey does report earnings for both full- and part-time employees, but it is easily skewed by higher-earning employees, given that it reflects an average rather than a median; furthermore, the CES excludes agricultural workers, a major sector of the workforce. The BLS also publishes the Quarterly Census of Employment and Wages (QCEW), which reports average wages for 95 percent of the workforce. Despite reporting detailed historical analysis at an industry and geographical level, notable deficiencies of the QCEW include (1) the six-month lag, limiting its usefulness for real-time decision-making, and (2) the reporting of average wages. Several yearly measures also report income and wages, but these do little to satisfy the need for real-time analysis of the workforce.

15   *Understanding the Status of American Workers Through Analysis of Current Population Survey Data* (Ludwig Institute for Shared Economic Prosperity, March 25, 2021), https://assets-global.website-files.com/63ba0d84fe573c7513595d6e/63c1bb3bca87e 7973a7d0f06_TWE White Paper.pdf.

16   "Consumer Price Index: Design," US Bureau of Labor Statistics, accessed February 6, 2025, https://www.bls.gov/opub/hom/cpi/design.htm.

17   "True Living Cost," Ludwig Institute for Shared Economic Prosperity, accessed February 6, 2025, https://www.lisep.org/tlc.

18   LISEP's "minimal quality of life" defines a standard of living reflective of the ideals of the American Dream: a vision of opportunity, upward mobility, and a fulfilling life for all who work hard. It incorporates the cost of basic needs as well as expenses associated with investments in life advancement and well-being such as education and cultural resources. For a more detailed explanation, see chapter 4.

19   Participants in the symposium included Dr. Robert Shiller; Dr. Larry Summers; Governor Deval Patrick; Dr. Daniel Markovits; Professor Mary Miller; Professor Steven Pearlstein; Sarah Bloom Raskin, former member of the Federal Reserve Board of Governors; Dr. Isabel Sawhill; Mayor Luke Bronin (Hartford); Dr. Oren Cass; Dr. Jacob Hacker; Dr. Glenn Hubbard; Dean Heather Gerken (Yale); Daryl Byrd, CEO of IberiaBank; Andrea Levere, president of Prosperity Now; Dr. Zach Liscow; Professor Jonathan Macey; Dr. Michael Moskow; Dr. Jay Shambaugh; Andrew Tisch, chairman of Loews Corporation; Dr. Susan Krause Bell; Professor Anika Singh Lemar; and David Newville, VP for Policy and Research at Prosperity Now.

Chapter 1

1   "Houston-Pasadena-The Woodlands, TX Metro Area," Census Reporter, accessed February 7, 2025, https://censusreporter.org/profiles/31000US26420-houston-the -woodlands-sugar-land-tx-metro-area/.

2   Center for American Progress, "Latino Workers Continue to Experience a Shortage of Good Jobs," July 18, 2022, https://www.americanprogress.org/article/latino-workers -continue-to-experience-a-shortage-of-good-jobs/.

3   E. Gregory and A. K. Miller, "Houston/Harris County Gender and Sexuality Data: Initial Report," *Sexuality, Gender & Policy* 3, no. 1 (2020): 8–22, https://doi.org/10 .1002/sgp2.12016; Steven Klineberg at al., *Shared Prospects: Hispanics and the Future of Houston: Findings from the Houston Surveys (1994–2014)* (Kinder Institute for Urban Research at Rice University, November 2014), https://rice.app.box.com/s /jpf0b8foh7dm3v54fqp4icfz6rhtgxpz.

4   Comprehensive methodological information, appendices, the latest LISEP metrics, and expert commentary pertaining to *The Mismeasurement of America* are available at www .lisep.org/mismeasurement.

5   To reflect the statistical method used in nationalized unemployment figures, the local unemployment rate referenced here differs from the Local Area Unemployment Statistics (LAUS) published by the BLS, which is not broken down by demographic groups. As with the annual national TRU, LISEP calculates the annual unemployment rate in the Houston Metropolitan Statistical Area (MSA) using the Current Population Survey (CPS) for each population. For the Houston MSA, the BLS uses an approach known as the "Handbook method" (see https://www.bls.gov/lau/laumthd.htm for more information) to estimate monthly employment and unemployment counts from additional data sources—notably, the Current Employment Statistics survey, the Quarterly Census of Employment and Wages, and unemployment claims—to mitigate volatility. For this reason, the annual estimates differ from the LISEP annual unemployment estimate, which uses the CPS.

6   The modern definition of unemployment (U-3) was implemented in the US Census Bureau's Enumerative Check Census in 1937. The "unemployed" are defined as those who were not working in the Census Week even though they were able to and were actively seeking work—in other words, simply everyone in the labor force who was not employed. David Card, "Origins of the Unemployment Rate: The Lasting Legacy of Measurement without Theory," *American Economic Review* 101, no. 3 (2011), 552–57.

7   "Labor Force Statistics from the Current Population Survey," US Bureau of Labor Statistics, accessed February 7, 2025, https://www.bls.gov/cps/cps_htgm.htm.

8   "True Rate of Unemployment," Ludwig Institute for Shared Economic Prosperity, accessed February 6, 2025, https://www.lisep.org/tru.

9   See www.lisep.org/mismeasurement for data and methodology used in the Houston TRU study.

10 Christopher Rugaber, "Small Businesses Find Tight Job Market Makes It Hard to Hire," *AP News*, August 7, 2018, https://apnews.com/general-news-1592cbc12ba04517aa52 c61f540f99d0; Rohit Arora, "Despite Rising Revenues, High Labor Costs Hurt Small Businesses," *Forbes*, July 9, 2023, https://www.forbes.com/sites/rohitarora/2023/07/08 /despite-rising-revenues-high-labor--costs-hurt-small-businesses/?sh=7ea52e0d5c4d.

11 In March 2024, the national U-3 stood at 3.8 percent, while the TRU was 24.2 percent—meaning that for every worker counted as unemployed by the BLS, 5.37 workers were functionally unemployed. Likewise, in 2023, 4.4 percent of Hispanic women in the United States were unemployed per the BLS, while 34.1 percent were functionally unemployed—meaning that for every unemployed Hispanic woman, 6.75 more were functionally unemployed.

12 Daniel A. Hartley, *Urban Decline in Rust-belt Cities* (Federal Reserve Bank of Cleveland, 2013), https://www.clevelandfed.org/publications/economic-commentary/2013/ec -201306-urban-decline-in-rust-belt-cities.

13 "True Rate of Unemployment," LISEP.

14 For this comparison, LISEP calculates the annual TRU and the average annual U-3 unemployment rate using the same method: by calculating the percentage of people in the labor force who were unemployed in a given year. At a local level, this has the advantage of mining a larger sample size to determine the year's average TRU and U-3. As a result, these estimates might differ slightly from the annual averages reported in other sources such as the Federal Reserve Economic Data (FRED) database, which computes the annual U-3 average as the average of each month's unemployment rate in a year. For example, FRED reports that the unemployment rate in 2023 in the United States was 3.6 percent, compared with the 3.5 percent reported in the context of this chapter. See www.lisep.org/mismeasurement for more details on the methodology. "Unemployment Rate (UNRATE)," BLS via Federal Reserve Bank of St. Louis, accessed May 23, 2024, https://fred.stlouisfed.org/series/UNRATE.

15 John H. Boyd et al., "The Stock Market's Reaction to Unemployment News, Stock-Bond Return Correlations, and the State of the Economy," *Journal of Investment Management* 4, no. 4 (2006): 73.

16   "Compilation and Release of Principal Federal Economic Indicators," *Federal Register* 50, no. 186 (Wednesday 25, 1985), Section 4, https://www.bea.gov/sites/default /files/2018-05/federalregister09251985.pdf.

17   "Changes to Department of Labor Media Lockup," US Bureau of Labor Statistics, accessed February 7, 2025, https://www.bls.gov/bls/changes-to-dol-media-lockup -effective-march-1-2020.htm.

18   Note that the late 1960s numbers of the share of part-time employment because of business conditions out of all employment are about 20 to 30 percent less than what they are now. Author's calculation based on: "Employment Level—Part-Time for Economic Reasons, Slack Work or Business Conditions, All Industries (LNS12032195)," BLS via Federal Reserve Bank of St. Louis, accessed April 5, 2024, https://fred.stlouis fed.org/series/LNS12032195. "Employment Level (CE16OV)," BLS via Federal Reserve Bank of St. Louis, accessed April 5, 2024, https://fred.stlouisfed.org/series/CE16OV.

19   Author's calculation of the share of employed workers who usually work part-time out of all employment. "Employed, Usually Work Part Time (LNS12600000)," Federal Reserve Bank of St. Louis, accessed February 7, 2025, https://fred.stlouisfed.org/series /LNS12600000; "Employment Level (CE16OV)," Federal Reserve Bank of St. Louis, accessed February 7, 2025, https://fred.stlouisfed.org/series/CE16OV; "1940: Population Labor Force Sample," US Census Bureau, accessed February 25, 2025, https://www2.census.gov/library/publications/decennial/1940/population-labor-force -sample/41236810p1.pdf (p. 12 shows that part-time work was much lower in 1940 than today, but says nothing about involuntary part-time or poverty wages).

20   Samantha Delouya, "2022 Had the Lowest Total Unemployment Rate Ever," CNN Business, December 20, 2023, https://www.cnn.com/2023/12/20/economy/lowest -unemployment-rate-year-2022/index.html.

21   Jeff Cox, "Federal Reserve Approves First Interest Rate Hike in More Than Three Years, Sees Six More Ahead," CNBC, March 16, 2022, https://www.cnbc.com/2022/03/16 /federal-reserve-meeting.html; Laura Rodini, "A Timeline of the Fed's '22–'23 Rate Hikes and What Caused Them," *The Street*, https://www.thestreet.com/fed/fed-rate -hikes-2022-2023-timeline-discussion#:~:text=Inpercent20Marchpercent202022percen t2Cpercent20thepercent20Fed,ratespercent20topercent205.25percentE2percent80 percent935.50percent25.

22   As stated previously, LISEP computed the annual U-3 for 2022 using a sample for the whole year to compare with the TRU rather than take the average of the monthly U-3 rates. Both methods yield very similar results, and coincidentally, in 2022, the national U-3 rate and the TRU rate would have been 3.6 percent and 23.4 percent as well, respectively, if taking the average of the monthly rates. For more details on the methodology, see www.lisep.org/mismeasurement.

23   The civilian labor force was 164.292 million in 2022, per "Civilian Labor Force Level (LNU01000000)," Federal Reserve Bank of St. Louis, accessed April 5, 2024, https ://fred.stlouisfed.org/series/LNU01000000; when multiplied by 0.234, this yields 38.444 million. When multiplied by the difference between the U-3 unemployment rate and the TRU of 0.198, it yields 32.530 million people who were functionally unemployed but uncounted by the BLS unemployment rate, on average.

24 "Unemployment Level (UNEMPLOY)," BLS via Federal Reserve Bank of St. Louis, accessed May 23, 2024, https://fred.stlouisfed.org/series/UNEMPLOY.

25 Violet Moya, "Sephora Never Valued Workers Like Me," *The New York Times*, April 18, 2020, https://www.nytimes.com/2020/04/18/opinion/sephora-layoffs-coronavirus.html.

26 The law specifically ensured that single women lost their benefits if they entered into employment. Linda Gordon and Felice Batlan, "The Legal History of the Aid to Dependent Children Program," Social Welfare History Project, 2011, https ://socialwelfare.library.vcu.edu/public-welfare/aid-to-dependent-children-the-legal -history/; Robert A. Moffitt, "The Effect of Welfare on Marriage and Fertility," chap. 4 in *Welfare, the Family, and Reproductive Behavior: Research Perspectives* (National Academies Press, 2011), https://www.ncbi.nlm.nih.gov/books/NBK230345/.

27 Janet L. Yellen, "So We All Can Succeed: 125 Years of Women's Participation in the Economy," speech, Brown University, May 5, 2017, transcript, https://www.federal reserve.gov/newsevents/speech/yellen20170505a.htm.

28 Evan K. Rose, "The Rise and Fall of Female Labor Force Participation during World War II in the United States," *Journal of Economic History* 78, no. 3 (2018): 673–711, accessed February 25, 2025, https://www.cambridge.org/core/journals/journal-of -economic-history/article/rise-and-fall-of-female-labor-force-participation-during -world-war-ii-in-the-united-states/66C7D7FD7F6424DF40625E913DDC788F; Yellen, "So We All Can Succeed."

29 Based on LISEP's calculation using Current Population Survey data from the Integrated Public Use Microdata Series (IPUMS) at https://cps.ipums.org/cps. We use the "whyptlw" (why part-time last week) variable to determine the 2023 percentages of part-time workers because of childcare obligations (3.48 percent) and because of childcare concerns (0.762 percent), or about 1.27 million workers. Sarah Flood et al., "Integrated Public Use Microdata Series, Current Population Survey: Version 11.0," [dataset], 2023, accessed April 29, 2024, https://doi.org/10.18128/D030.V11.0. More on these calculations at www.lisep.org/mismeasurement.

30 "All Employees, Manufacturing (MANEMP)," BLS via Federal Reserve Bank of St. Louis, accessed February 27, 2025, https://fred.stlouisfed.org/series/MANEMP.

31 Andre Barbe and David Riker, "The Effects of Offshoring on US Workers; A Review of the Literature," *Journal of International Commerce and Economics* (June 2018), https ://www.usitc.gov/publications/332/journals/offshoring_and_labor_final.pdf; Daron Acemoglu and Pascual Restrepo, *Robots and Jobs: Evidence from US Labor Markets* (National Bureau of Economic Research, 2017), https://www.nber.org/system/files /working_papers/w23285/w23285.pdf.

32 "Production, Sales, Work Started and Orders: Production Volume: Economic Activity: Manufacturing for United States (PRMNTO01USQ661N)," Organization for Economic Co-operation and Development via Federal Reserve Bank of St. Louis, accessed May 21, 2024, https://fred.stlouisfed.org/series/PRMNTO01USQ661N; "All Employees, Manufacturing (MANEMP)," BLS via Federal Reserve Bank of St. Louis, accessed May 23, 2024; "Employment Level (CE16OV)," BLS via Federal Reserve Bank of St. Louis, accessed May 23, 2024, https://fred.stlouisfed.org/series/CE16OV.

33 Chris Tilly, "Reasons for the Continuing Growth of Part-Time Employment," *Monthly Labor Review*, March 1991, 14, https://www.bls.gov/opub/mlr/1991/03/art2full.pdf.

34   In 1979, 21.2 percent of private-sector workers were union members and 23.2 percent were covered by unions. Respectively those numbers were 6.0 percent and 6.8 percent in 2023. See Barry Hirsch et al., "Union Membership, Coverage, and Earnings from the CPS," January 16, 2024, http://www.unionstats.com/; "Union Members—2024," US Bureau of Labor Statistics, January 28, 2025, https://www.bls.gov/news.release/pdf /union2.pdf.

35   Hirsch, "Union Membership"; "Union Members—2024," BLS.

36   "Labor Force Statistics from the Current Population Survey," US Bureau of Labor Statistics, accessed February 25, 2025, https://www.bls.gov/cps/data/aa2023 /cpsaat11b.htm.

37   Mack Ott, "The Growing Share of Services in the U.S. Economy—Degeneration or Evolution?," *Review* (Federal Reserve Bank of St. Louis) 69, no. 6 (June/July 1987): 5–22, https://doi.org/10.20955/r.69.5-22.bzk.

38   "Where Did All The Pensions Go?," *Forbes*, April 4, 2018, https://www.forbes.com /sites/impactpartners/2018/02/09/where-did-all-the-pensions-go/?sh=7060504a3aab.

39   Dan Rosenzweig-Ziff, "The Autoworker Strikes That Changed America," *The Washington Post*, September 16, 2023, https://www.washingtonpost.com/history/2023/09/16/uaw -major-strikes-history/.

40   Tilly, "Reasons for the Continuing Growth"; Daniel Flaming et al., *Hungry at the Table: White Paper on Grocery Workers at the Kroger Company* (Economic Roundtable, January 11, 2022), https://economicrt.org/publication/hungry-at-the-table/.

41   "Employee Benefits in the United States—March 2024," US Bureau of Labor Statistics, accessed February 7, 2025, https://www.bls.gov/news.release/pdf/ebs2.pdf.

42   "Employers aren't required to provide health insurance for part-time employees, even if they provide coverage for full-time employees," per "Health Insurance If You Work Part-time," HealthCare.gov, accessed February 7, 2025, https://www.healthcare.gov/ part-time-workers/; "Any employee who works an average of at least 30 hours per week for more than 120 days in a year. Part-time employees work an average of less than 30 hours per week," per "Full-time Employee (FTE)," HealthCare.gov, accessed February 7, 2025, https://www.healthcare.gov/glossary/full-time-employee/. Note that this differs from the BLS and LISEP definition of a part-time worker who works fewer than thirty-five hours a week.

43   David Siders, "Why Democrats Stopped Stressing over Big Spending," Politico, May 10, 2021, https://www.politico.com/news/2021/05/10/democrats-big-government-spending -485209; Margo Sanger-Katz, "Little-Known Part of GOP Bill Could 'Make It Impossible to Regulate," *The New York Times*, May 12, 2023, https://www.nytimes.com /2023/05/12/upshot/republican-bill-government-regulations.html.

44   Sahil Kapur and Leigh Ann Caldwell, "Congress Is Moving to Another Round of Coronavirus Relief. Here Are the Battle Lines," NBC News, May 22, 2020, https ://www.nbcnews.com/politics/congress/congress-moving-another-round-coronavirus -relief-here-are-battle-lines-n1212486.

45   "History," US House Committee on the Budget, accessed February 7, 2025, https ://budget.house.gov/about/history.

46   "Real Gross Domestic Product (GDPC1)," BLS via Federal Reserve Bank of St. Louis, accessed May 23, 2024, https://fred.stlouisfed.org/series/GDPC1.

47   "SNP - Free Realtime Quote," Yahoo Finance, accessed February 25, 2025, https://finance.yahoo.com/quote/%5EGSPC/history/?.

48   Refers to the first quarter of 2018. "Unemployment Rate (UNRATE)," BLS via Federal Reserve Bank of St. Louis, accessed February 25, 2025, https://fred.stlouisfed.org/series/UNRATE.

49   The requested budget amount (in thousands of dollars) for fiscal year 2019 was $1,296,938; the continuing resolution for fiscal year 2018 was $1,692,581. See Row E., "Total, Estimated Obligations," *FY 2019 Congressional Budget Justification Employment and Training Administration*, Job Corps: JC-3, https://www.dol.gov/sites/dolgov/files/general/budget/2019/CBJ-2019-V1-04.pdf.

50   "Trump Administration to Pull Out of Job Corps Program, Laying Off 1,100 Workers," *The Washington Post*, May 25, 2019, https://www.washingtonpost.com/politics/trump-administration-to-pull-out-of-rural-job-corps-program-laying-off-1100-federal-workers/2019/05/24/b93c5af4-7e5b-11e9-8bb7-0fc796cf2ec0_story.html.

Chapter 2

1   The wage premium for undesirable work does not always hold, but it does hold more often than not; see Peter Dorman and Les Boden, *Risk without Reward: The Myth of Wage Compensation for Hazardous Work* (Economic Policy Institute), April 19, 2021, https://www.epi.org/unequalpower/publications/risk-without-reward-the-myth-of-wage-compensation-for-hazardous-work/. For construction workers, the premium does hold, bringing a higher weekly income than for those employed in other blue-collar industries; see "Average Hourly Wages for Blue Collar Occupations across Levels, Worker Characteristics, and Geographic Location," US Bureau of Labor Statistics, accessed February 7, 2025, https://www.bls.gov/mwe/factsheets/blue-collar-jobs-factsheet.htm; "Usual Weekly Earnings of Wage and Salary Workers: First Quarter 2024," US Bureau of Labor Statistics, April 16, 2024, https://www.bls.gov/news.release/archives/wkyeng_04162024.pdf (Table 4 indicates in the first quarter of 2024, real wages for construction workers outpaced those of production workers by 11 percent).

2   "Occupational Outlook Handbook: How to Become a Teller," US Bureau of Labor Statistics, accessed February 7, 2025, https://www.bls.gov/ooh/office-and-administrative-support/tellers.htm#tab-4; "Occupational Outlook Handbook: How to Become a Loan Officer," US Bureau of Labor Statistics, accessed February 7, 2025, https://www.bls.gov/ooh/business-and-financial/loan-officers.htm#tab-4.

3   "Occupational Outlook Handbook: How to Become a Roofer," US Bureau of Labor Statistics, accessed February 25, 2025, https://www.bls.gov/ooh/construction-and-extraction/roofers.htm#tab-4.

4   Troy Gilchrist and Bart Hobijn, "The Divergent Signals about Labor Market Slack," Federal Reserve Bank of San Francisco, June 1, 2021, https://www.frbsf.org/research-and-insights/publications/economic-letter/2021/06/divergent-signals-about-labor-market-slack-covid-19/.

5   "Overview of BLS Wage Data by Area and Occupation," US Bureau of Labor Statistics, accessed February 7, 2025, https://www.bls.gov/bls/blswage.htm#Metropolitan.

6   "Economic News Release: Usual Weekly Earnings of Wage and Salary Workers," US
      Bureau of Labor Statistics, accessed February 7, 2025, https://www.bls.gov/news.release
      /wkyeng.toc.htm.

7   Brendan Duke, "Workers' Paychecks Are Growing More Quickly Than Prices," Center
      for American Progress, January 3, 2024, https://www.americanprogress.org/article
      /workers-paychecks-are-growing-more-quickly-than-prices/; J. Arky, "Here's How Much
      the Living Wage Is in Your State," Nasdaq, April 21, 2024, https://www.nasdaq.com
      /articles/heres-how-much-the-living-wage-is-in-your-state?time=1713700821.

8   Quarterly averaged TRU from the first to the second quarters of 2020. For this chapter,
      LISEP computes the average of the seasonally adjusted TRUs for the three months
      of each quarter to correspond with the same timeline used for the wages metrics. The
      national monthly sample size in the Current Population Survey is large enough for
      our purposes, and avoids going back to the microdata. "True Rate of Unemployment,"
      Ludwig Institute for Shared Economic Prosperity, accessed June 1, 2024, https://www
      .lisep.org/tru; "True Weekly Earnings," Ludwig Institute for Shared Economic
      Prosperity, accessed February 7, 2025, https://www.lisep.org/twe; "Employed Full
      Time: Median Usual Weekly Real Earnings: Wage and Salary Workers: 16 Years and
      Over (LES1252881600Q)," BLS via Federal Reserve Bank of St. Louis, accessed
      February 26, 2025, https://fred.stlouisfed.org/series/LES1252881600Q.

9   Cecilia Rouse and Martha Gimbel, "The Pandemic's Effect on Measured Wage
      Growth," WhiteHouse.gov, April 19, 2021, https://bidenwhitehouse.archives.gov/cea
      /written-materials/2021/04/19/the-pandemics-effect-on-measured-wage-growth/;
      "Usual Weekly Earnings of Wage and Salary Workers: Fourth Quarter 2024," US
      Bureau of Labor Statistics, January 22, 2025, 1, https://www.bls.gov/news.release
      /archives/wkyeng_01222025.pdf.

10   Serdar Birinci and Aaron Amburgey, "How Job Separations Differed between the Great
      Recession and COVID-19 Recession," Federal Reserve Bank of St. Louis, June 22,
      2021, https://www.stlouisfed.org/on-the-economy/2021/june/job-separations-differed
      -between-recessions.

11   A 2015 study from the US Government Accountability Office found that contingent
      workers, defined as those in temporary or alternative work arrangements, earned
      10.6 percent less on an hourly basis than similar "standard" workers did. "Contingent
      Workforce: Size, Characteristics, Earnings, and Benefits," US Government
      Accountability Office, May 20, 2015, https://www.gao.gov/products/gao-15-168r.

12   The December 2007–June 2009 dates were selected because they correspond to the
      Great Recession as defined by the National Bureau of Economic Research. See "All
      Employees, Total Nonfarm (PAYEMS)," BLS via Federal Reserve Bank of St. Louis,
      accessed April 19, 2024, https://fred.stlouisfed.org/series/PAYEMS; "All Employees,
      Temporary Help Services (TEMPHELPS)," BLS via Federal Reserve Bank of St. Louis,
      accessed April 19, 2024, https://fred.stlouisfed.org/series/TEMPHELPS.

13   The BLS's median usual real weekly earnings metric for wage and salaried workers
      employed full-time rose 3.9 percent between the last quarter of 2007 and the second
      quarter of 2009. "Employed Full Time: Median Usual Weekly Real Earnings: Wage
      and Salary Workers: 16 Years and Over (LES1252881600Q)," BLS via Federal Reserve
      Bank of St. Louis, accessed April 16, 2024, https://fred.stlouisfed.org/series
      /LES1252881600Q.

14   Author's calculations are based on BLS's Table 6 that lists median usual weekly earnings; press releases throughout time show that median earnings for exclusively part-time workers fall during recessions. "Economic News Release: Table 6, Median Usual Weekly Earnings of Part-Time Wage and Salary Workers by Selected Characteristics, Quarterly Averages, Not Seasonally Adjusted," US Bureau of Labor Statistics, accessed February 7, 2025. See www.lisep.org/mismeasurement for more details.

15   "Employed, Usually Work Part Time (LNS12600000)," Federal Reserve Bank of St. Louis, accessed February 7, 2025, https://fred.stlouisfed.org/series/LNS12600000; "Employment Level (CE16OV)," Federal Reserve Bank of St. Louis, accessed February 7, 2025, https://fred.stlouisfed.org/series/CE16OV.

16   The IPUMS Annual Social and Economic Supplement (ASEC) dataset and author's calculations indicate that the bottom half of wage earners (measured by hourly income) has double the prevalence of part-time workers in 2022 (40 percent compared with 20 percent). Unfortunately, even this measure is a lower estimate because the data measures only workers on hourly rates, not salaried workers. Checking robustness by calculating all workers' total income, the takeaways are starker. (Disclaimer: This is not a perfect check because part-time workers achieve fewer working hours, so it is unsurprising that they would be in the lower half of the distribution.) In this case, the part-time worker prevalence is nearly six times as great with workers in the bottom half versus the top half of income earners (37.6 percent versus 6.9 percent in 2022). See www.lisep.org/mismeasurement for calculations.

17   The research is conducted using the IPUMS ASEC. The occupations are based on the Census Bureau's 2010 occupation classification scheme: Hostesses and hosts are in occupation classification code 4150, waiters and waitresses in 4110, and dental hygienists in 3310. Although the percentages are listed for 2022, they are stable throughout time. See www.lisep.org/mismeasurement for information on calculation and data history.

18   Author's calculation based on: "Employment Level—Part-Time for Economic Reasons, Slack Work or Business Conditions, All Industries (LNS12032195)," BLS via Federal Reserve Bank of St. Louis, accessed April 5, 2024, https://fred.stlouisfed.org/series /LNS12032195; "Employment Level (CE16OV)," BLS via Federal Reserve Bank of St. Louis, accessed April 5, 2024, https://fred.stlouisfed.org/series/CE16OV.

19   Lonnie Golden, "Part-Time Workers Pay a Big-Time Penalty," Economic Policy Institute, February 27, 2020, https://www.epi.org/publication/part-time-pay-penalty/.

20   In 2022, 33.5 percent of construction workers were the sole providers for their family. Author's calculations are based on the IPUMS ASEC; see www.lisep.org/mismeasurement for details. See also Sarah Flood et al., "Integrated Public Use Microdata Series, Current Population Survey: Version 11.0" [dataset], 2023, accessed April 29, 2024, https://doi .org/10.18128/D030.V11.0.

21   The difference between the BLS usual weekly earnings metric and LISEP's TWE
     fluctuates over time based on labor market characteristics such as the degree of slack.
     Between the first quarter of 1982 (when the first weekly earnings measures were
     available) and the first quarter of 2024, the TWE was 19.2 percent lower than the
     headline BLS median earnings statistic on average. At the time of writing, the TWE was
     16.6 percent lower than the BLS metric as of the first quarter of 2024. "True Weekly
     Earnings," Ludwig Institute for Shared Economic Prosperity, accessed May 28, 2024,
     https://www.lisep.org/twe.

22   When using the real average hourly earnings (another earnings metric that is
     commonly cited), this also misses the recession, both in total earnings (jumped
     more than 3 percent from the fourth quarter of 2007 to the second quarter of
     2009) and in the construction sector (jumped almost 5 percent)—in contrast to
     the TWE numbers, which fell. US Bureau of Labor Statistics, "Average Hourly
     Earnings of All Employees, 1982–1984 dollars, Total Private, Seasonally Adjusted
     (CES0500000013)," accessed February 26, 2025; US Bureau of Labor Statistics,
     "Average Hourly Earnings of All Employees, 1982–1984 dollars, Construction,
     Seasonally Adjusted (CES2000000013)," accessed February 26, 2025; "Employed Full
     Time: Median Usual Weekly Real Earnings: Wage and Salary Workers: 16 Years and
     Over (LES1252881600Q)," BLS via Federal Reserve Bank of St. Louis, accessed April
     16, 2024, https://fred.stlouisfed.org/series/LES1252881600Q.

23   "New One Family Houses Sold: United States (HSN1F)," US Census Bureau and
     US Department of Housing and Urban Development via Federal Reserve Bank of St.
     Louis, accessed February 7, 2025, https://fred.stlouisfed.org/series/HSN1F.

24   "Real Gross Domestic Product: Construction (23) in the United States
     (USCONSTRGSP)," US Bureau of Economic Analysis via Federal Reserve Bank of St.
     Louis, accessed February 26, 2025, https://fred.stlouisfed.org/series/USCONSTRGSP.

25   John V. Duca, "Subprime Mortgage Crisis: 2007–2010," Federal Reserve History,
     November 22, 2013, https://www.federalreservehistory.org/essays/subprime-mortgage
     -crisis.

26   Gloria Guzman and Melissa Kollar, "Income in the United States: 2022," US Census
     Bureau, September 12, 2023, https://www.census.gov/library/publications/2023
     /demo/p60-279.html#:~:text=Highlights,andpercent20Tablepercent20Apercent2D1.

27   Correlation is based off of yearly TWE and household median income. "Real Median
     Household Income in the United States (MEHOINUSA672N)," US Census Bureau
     via Federal Reserve of St. Louis, accessed February 7, 2025, https://fred.stlouisfed.org
     /series/MEHOINUSA672N; "True Weekly Earnings," Ludwig Institute for Shared
     Economic Prosperity, accessed May 23, 2024, https://www.lisep.org/twe. See www
     .lisep.org/mismeasurement for calculations.

28   "True Rate of Unemployment," Ludwig Institute for Shared Economic Prosperity,
     accessed February 6, 2025, https://www.lisep.org/tru.

Chapter 3

1   The year 2018 is used here as the benchmark for when these conversations were representative of the broader national dialogue described in our writing. *The Vanishing American Dream*, edited by Gene Ludwig (p. 56), reports these interviews as taking place after publication of *The Forgotten Americans*, by Isabel Sawhill, in September 2018. A slight variation in both wording and timing occurs in Dr. Sawhill's October 2018 Brookings article "What the Forgotten Americans Really Want—and How to Give It to Them" (https://www.brookings.edu/articles/what-the-forgotten-americans -really-want-and-how-to-give-it-to-them/), which references a woman describing herself as part of the "holding-on-by-your fingernails" class during an interview conducted as part of Dr. Sawhill's 2016–2018 research.

2   This specifically refers to cash income. Tracey Farrigan, "Poverty and Deep Poverty Increasing in Rural America," US Department of Agriculture Economic Research Service, March 4, 2014, https://www.ers.usda.gov/amber-waves/2014/march/poverty -and-deep-poverty-increasing-in-rural-america.

3   "Part V: Conclusion," in *Chart Book: Tracking the Post-Great Recession Economy*, Center on Budget and Policy Priorities, May 27, 2022, https://www.cbpp.org/research /economy/tracking-the-post-great-recession-economy.

4   The S&P closed at 2,695.81 on January 2, 2018, versus closing at 931.80 on January 2, 2009. "S&P 500 (^GSPC) Stock Historical Prices & Data," Yahoo Finance, accessed February 7, 2025, https://finance.yahoo.com/quote/percent5EGSPC/history/?period 1=1230768000&period2=1514937600.

5   Ruth Igielnik and Kim Parker, "Most Americans Say the Current Economy Is Helping the Rich, Hurting the Poor and Middle Class," Pew Research Center, December 11, 2019, https://www.pewresearch.org/social-trends/2019/12/11/most-americans-say-the -current-economy-is-helping-the-rich-hurting-the-poor-and-middle-class/.

6   *A Quarterly Tracking Poll of Middle-Income Americans' Financial Mood* (Primerica, October 2023), https://www.primerica.com/public/Fact_Sheet_Primerica_Financial _Security_Monitor_Q3_2023.pdf.

7   *Winning Back Working America: A PPI/YouGov Survey of Working-Class Attitudes* (Progressive Policy Institute, November 2023), https://www.progressivepolicy.org /wp-content/uploads/2023/11/PPI-Winning-Back-Working-America-Poll.pdf.

8   The poverty rate tracked by the US Census Bureau is the Supplemental Poverty Measure, which does include non-cash benefits like nutritional assistance, so SNAP benefits are considered. The EITC, Social Security benefits, and SNAP have been found to reduce child poverty. Linda Fox and Kalee Burns, "What's the Difference Between Supplemental and Official Poverty Measures?," US Census Bureau, September 9, 2021, https://www.census.gov/newsroom/blogs/random-samplings/2021/09/difference -between-supplemental-and-official-poverty-measures.html; Dana Thomson et al., *Lessons From a Historic Decline in Child Poverty* (Child Trends, 2022), 43, https://www .childtrends.org/publications/lessons-from-a-historic-decline-in-child-poverty.

9   Megan Brenan, "Economic Mood Improves, but Inflation Still Vexing Americans," Gallup, January 30, 2024, https://news.gallup.com/poll/609221/economic-mood -improves-inflation-vexing-americans.aspx.

10 Patrick Murray, "Half Say Middle Class Not Benefiting at All from Biden Policies," Monmouth University Poll, April 11, 2023, https://www.monmouth.edu/polling -institute/reports/monmouthpoll_us_041123/.

11 Vishwa Bhatt, "Two in Three Battleground Constituents Support Policies Aimed at Growing the Middle Class," Navigator, August 2, 2023, https://navigatorresearch.org /two-in-three-battleground-constituents-support-policies-aimed-at-growing-the-middle -class/.

12 German Lopez, "The Past Year of Research Has Made It Very Clear: Trump Won Because of Racial Resentment," Vox, December 15, 2017, https://www.vox.com /identities/2017/12/15/16781222/trump-racism-economic-anxiety-study.

13 Dan Froomkin, "Political Journalists Are Doing Voter Interviews All Wrong," Press Watch, October 19, 2019, https://presswatchers.org/2019/10/political-journalists -are-doing-voter-interviews-all-wrong/; Edward Lempinen, "Loss, Fear and Rage: Are White Men Rebelling Against Democracy?," UC Berkeley News, https://news.berkeley .edu/2022/11/14/loss-fear-and-rage-are-white-men-rebelling-against-democracy.

14 Lopez, "The Past Year of Research"; John Blake, "This Is What 'Whitelash' Looks Like," CNN, November 19, 2016, https://www.cnn.com/2016/11/11/us/obama-trump -white-backlash/index.html.

15 After a rise starting in 2021, online search interest for the term "inflation" between 2004 and 2023 peaked around August 2022, and then hovered at around half that peak. From 2004 to 2020, that high point was closer to one-fourth, and the value never exceeded 33 percent of the search interest it would attain in 2022. See Google Trends (https://www.google.com/trends).

16 "Consumer Price Index: Design," US Bureau of Labor Statistics, accessed February 6, 2025, https://www.bls.gov/opub/hom/cpi/design.htm.

17 The Federal Reserve tends to target the Personal Consumption Expenditures (PCE) index for its chosen inflation index, although it does monitor other price indexes. The PCE is measured by the Department of Commerce through the Bureau of Economic Analysis (BEA), whereas the CPI is measured by the Department of Labor through the Bureau of Labor Statistics. The differences between the two indexes fall largely into four categories. First, they are calculated on different aggregation formulas; in theory, the formula for the PCE more comprehensively accounts for price changes. Second, different weights are used, with the CPI estimating weights based on the Consumer Expenditure Survey and the PCE using weights from various business surveys. Third, the CPI most commonly published and referred to is the CPI-U, which estimates price changes only for urban households, whereas the PCE attempts to measure all households as well as nonprofit institutions serving households. Finally, there is a mix of other effects, including "seasonal adjustment differences, price differences, and residual differences"—the largest of which, in practice, is seasonal adjustment. "What Is Inflation and How Does the Federal Reserve Measure It?," Board of Governors of the Federal Reserve System, accessed February 8, 2025, https://www.federalreserve.gov /faqs/5CD8134B130A43E998A945450E041BF0.htm; "Consumer Price Index, First Quarter 2011," Focus on Prices and Spending 2, no. 3 (May 2011), US Bureau of Labor Statistics, https://www.bls.gov/opub/btn/archive/differences-between-the-consumer -price-index-and-the-personal-consumption-expenditures-price-index.pdf.

18   Stephen B. Reed and Kenneth J. Stewart, "Why Does BLS Provide Both the CPI-W and CPI-U?," *Beyond the Numbers* (blog), US Bureau of Labor Statistics, February 28, 2014, https://www.bls.gov/opub/btn/volume-3/why-does-bls-provide-both-the-cpi-w-and-cpi-u.htm; "Consumer Price Index for All Urban Consumers: All Items in US City Average (CPIAUCSL)," BLS via Federal Reserve Bank of St. Louis, accessed April 24, 2024, https://fred.stlouisfed.org/series/CPIAUCSL; "Consumer Price Index for All Urban Wage Earners and Clerical Workers: All Items in US City Average (CWUR0000SA0)," BLS via Federal Reserve Bank of St. Louis, accessed April 24, 2024, https://fred.stlouisfed.org/series/CWUR0000SA0.

19   BLS statisticians have published one-off papers to determine different CPIs for lower- and higher-income households, but historically have not regularly published an index. See, for example, Josh Klick and Anya Stockburger, *Experimental CPI for Lower and Higher Income Households* (US Bureau of Labor Statistics, Office of Prices and Living Conditions, March 8, 2021), https://www.bls.gov/osmr/research-papers/2021/pdf/ec 210030.pdf. However, recognizing the increased "user demand for CPIs across the income distribution," the BLS plans to release research CPI by equivalized income quintiles (R-CPI-I) and research chained CPI by equivalized income quintiles (R-C-CPI-I) semiannually. More information on this endeavor is available at www.bls.gov /cpi/research-series/r-cpi-i.htm.

20   "Consumer Price Index: Concepts," US Bureau of Labor Statistics, accessed February 8, 2025, https://www.bls.gov/opub/hom/cpi/concepts.htm.

21   The CPI-U for shelter, which is included in the CPI-U index for housing, focuses specifically on the service that a housing unit provides its occupants (e.g. rent, owners' equivalent rent, and housing insurance), and also rose 90 percent over that time period. The CPI-U index for housing also includes costs such as utilities, household maintenance, furniture, and appliances in addition to rent. For further details on the goods and services that make up the housing aggregate, see "Appendix 2. Content of CPI Entry Level Items," US Bureau of Labor Statistics, accessed February 26, 2025, https://www.bls.gov/cpi/additional-resources/entry-level-item-descriptions .htm. "Consumer Price Index for All Urban Consumers: Shelter in US City Average (CUSR0000SAH1)," BLS via Federal Reserve Bank of St. Louis, December 11, 2024, https://fred.stlouisfed.org/series/CUSR0000SAH1; "Consumer Price Index: Design— Shelter," US Bureau of Labor Statistics, accessed February 7, 2025, https://www.bls .gov/opub/hom/cpi/design.htm#shelter; "Consumer Price Index for All Urban Consumers: Housing in US City Average (CPIHOSNS)," BLS via Federal Reserve Bank of St. Louis, accessed December 11, 2024, https://fred.stlouisfed.org/series/CPIHOSNS.

22   "S&P CoreLogic Case-Shiller US National Home Price Index (CSUSHPINSA)," BLS via Federal Reserve Bank of St. Louis, December 11, 2024, https://fred.stlouisfed.org /series/CSUSHPINSA.

23   "Consumer Price Index for All Urban Consumers: Medical Care Services in US City Average (CUSR0000SAM2)," BLS via Federal Reserve Bank of St. Louis, December 9, 2024, https://fred.stlouisfed.org/series/CUSR0000SAM2.

24   "True Living Cost," Ludwig Institute for Shared Economic Prosperity, accessed February 26, 2025, https://www.lisep.org/tlc.

25   The BLS recognizes that "medical insurance premiums constitute the largest part of consumers' out-of-pocket spending for medical care" but does not try to measure this; instead, "the CPI allocates most of consumers' out-of-pocket expenditures on health insurance premiums to the weights for other health care services and commodities, placing the small remainder, which covers the insurance companies' costs and their profits, into a separate stratum." US Bureau of Labor Statistics, "Chapter 17: The Consumer Price Index," *Handbook of Methods*, updated February 14, 2018, https ://www.bls.gov/opub/hom/pdf/cpi-20180214.pdf.

26   Watches have a weight of 0.041, and jewelry has a weight of 0.197, so their combined weight is 0.238 in 2023. Rice and pasta are grouped together and have a weight of 0.139 (as of February 2024). "Consumer Price Index: Table 1 (2022 Weights). Relative importance of components in the Consumer Price Indexes: US City Average, December 2023," US Bureau of Labor Statistics, accessed February 8, 2025, https ://www.bls.gov/cpi/tables/relative-importance/2023.htm.

27   Second homes have a weight of 1.329. As of February 2024, bread has a weight of 0.203, pork is 0.328, eggs are 0.119, milk is 0.178, chicken is 0.254, and potatoes are 0.073, so all food items combined have a weight of 1.155. "Consumer Price Index: Table 1 (2022 Weights)," BLS.

28   Based on the annual average of the following non-seasonally adjusted series: airline fares, CUUS0000SETG01; ground beef, CUUS0000SEFC01; bread, CUUS0000SEFB01; new cars, CUUS0000SS45011; used cars, CUUS0000SETA02; jewelry, CUUS0000SEAG02. The series were accessed on December 11, 2024, https ://www.bls.gov/cpi/data.htm.

29   For specific details on the design of the TLC, reference the methodology accessible at Philip Cornell et al., *True Living Cost (TLC) Index Methodology* (Ludwig Institute for Shared Economic Prosperity, revised December 19, 2024), https://cdn.prod.website -files.com/63ba0d84fe573c7513595d6e/676447106cd0fca2802b6a53_LISEP _True%20Living%20Cost%20Methodology_December%202024.pdf.

30   Peter Mateyka and Jayne Yoo, "Low-Income Renters Spent Larger Share of Income on Rent in 2021," US Census Bureau, March 2, 2023, https://www.census.gov/library /stories/2023/03/low-income-renters-spent-larger-share-of-income-on-rent.html#:~:text =Renterpercent2Doccupiedpercent20householdspercent20madepercent20up,were percent20inpercent20renterpercent2Doccupiedpercent20units.

31   "Consumer Price Index for All Urban Consumers: Medical Care in US City Average (CPIMEDSL)," BLS via Federal Reserve Bank of St. Louis, accessed May 29, 2024, https://fred.stlouisfed.org/series/CPIMEDSL. Between 2001 and 2022, the cost for medical care rose by 194 percent as tracked by the TLC, compared with just 100 percent according to the CPI-U.

32   Specifically, LISEP estimates the true living costs for eight family types based on the number of adults (one or two) and children (ranging from none to three) since household needs and costs vary based on the number of adults and children present. Both adults are assumed to be working full-time. More at https://www.lisep.org/tlc.

33   "Minutes of the Federal Open Market Committee," the Federal Reserve Board, June
      29–30, 2004, https://www.federalreserve.gov/fomc/minutes/20040630.htm; Ben S.
      Bernanke, "The Crisis and the Policy Response," Board of Governors of the Federal
      Reserve System, January 13, 2009, https://www.federalreserve.gov/newsevents/speech
      /bernanke20090113a.htm; "Minutes of the Federal Open Market Committee,"
      November 2–3, 2010, https://www.federalreserve.gov/monetarypolicy/fomcminutes
      20101103.htm.

34   97.4 divided by 72.1 equals 135.1 percent, meaning that 97.4 is 35.1 percent larger than
      72.1. The difference in percentage points is calculated by subtracting 72.1 percent from
      97.4 percent, which equals 25.3 percentage points. "True Living Cost," Ludwig Institute
      for Shared Economic Prosperity, accessed February 9, 2025, https://www.lisep.org/tlc.

35   Author's calculations are based on CPS outgoing rotational group supplement. LISEP
      uses the 2010 Occupational Code classification scheme from the US Census Bureau,
      with codes 3740, 3130, and 7150 representing firefighters, nurses, and auto mechanics,
      respectively. When testing for robustness using the ASEC, we find similar results:
      changes of 78 percent, 67 percent, and 67 percent in nominal annual earnings for
      nurses, firefighters, and auto mechanics, respectively, from 2001 to 2022.

36   "Defined benefit pension plans provide employees with guaranteed retirement
      benefits based on benefit formulas. A participant's retirement age, length of service,
      and preretirement earnings may affect the benefits received," per US Bureau of Labor
      Statistics, "National Compensation Measures: Concepts," *Handbook of Methods*,
      updated December 15, 2017, https://www.bls.gov/opub/hom/ncs/concepts.htm. See
      also Patrick W. Seburn, "Evolutions of Employer-Provided Defined Benefit Pensions,"
      Monthly Labor Review, December 1991, 16–23, https://www.bls.gov/mlr/1991/12
      /art3full.pdf; Barbara A. Butrica et al., "The Disappearing Defined Benefit Pension
      and Its Potential Impact on the Retirement Incomes of Baby Boomers," *Social Security
      Bulletin* 69, no. 3 (2009), https://www.ssa.gov/policy/docs/ssb/v69n3/v69n3p1.html.

37   "Where Did All The Pensions Go?," *Forbes*, February 9, 2018, https://www.forbes.com
      /sites/impactpartners/2018/02/09/where-did-all-the-pensions-go/?sh=7060504a3aab.

38   Calculations were made from the EBS survey—specifically, series NBU19000000
      000000026291, NBU19000002520000026291, NBU19000003300000026291, and
      NBU19000002911110026291. "Employee Benefits," US Bureau of Labor Statistics,
      accessed December 12, 2024, https://www.bls.gov/ebs/.

39   This corresponds to a pension for someone on an E-8 pay grade with over twenty-
      six years of service, earning $3,467.10 a month, and resulting in an initial pension
      payment of $2,600 given a 75 percent pay multiplier. "Military Pay Chart 2000: 2000
      Officer Basic Military Pay Chart," Navy Cyber Space, accessed February 9, 2025,
      https://www.navycs.com/charts/2000-military-pay-chart.html#officer-pay-chart;
      "Military Compensation," Military Pay, accessed February 9, 2025, https://militarypay
      .defense.gov/Pay/Retirement/.

40   See author's calculation at www.lisep.org/mismeasurement. For all calculations using the
      CPI-W, the data is sourced from "Consumer Price Index for All Urban Wage Earners and
      Clerical Workers: All Items in US City Average (CWUR0000SA0)," April 26, 2024, BLS
      via Federal Reserve Bank of St. Louis, https://fred.stlouisfed.org/series/CWUR0000SA0.

41   "Eligibility for Social Security in Retirement," Social Security Administration, accessed February 9, 2025, https://www.ssa.gov/retirement/eligibility.

42   In theory, Social Security follows a similar model as other defined benefit pension funds, where current employee contributions and returns on invested securities finance the current benefit payments. In practice, because Social Security is running on an income deficit—meaning its annual payments are greater than its income—payroll taxes (which currently account for over 90 percent of Social Security's fund income) fund the vast majority of outgoing payments. The rest is financed through income taxes on Social Security benefits, earned interest on the fund's assets, and asset reserves. "How Is Social Security Financed?," Social Security Administration (Press Office), accessed February 9, 2025, https://www.ssa.gov/news/press/factsheets/HowAreSocialSecurity .htm; "Summary: Actuarial Status of the Social Security Trust Funds," Social Security Administration, May 2024, https://www.ssa.gov/policy/trust-funds-summary.html.

43   See author's calculation at www.lisep.org/mismeasurement.

44   Poverty thresholds are issued by the Census Bureau and used for statistical purposes (e.g., determining how many people live in poverty), updated annually based on the CPI-U. Poverty guidelines, or poverty "lines," are issued by the Department of Health and Human Services and represent a simplified version of the poverty thresholds used to determine financial eligibility for certain programs. In other words, the poverty guidelines are determined by the poverty thresholds. "Frequently Asked Questions Related to the Poverty Guidelines and Poverty," Office of the Assistant Secretary for Planning and Evaluation, accessed February 9, 2025, https://aspe.hhs.gov/topics /poverty-economic-mobility/poverty-guidelines/frequently-asked-questions-related -poverty-guidelines-poverty. "Programs That Use the Poverty Guidelines as a Part of Eligibility Determination," US Department of Health and Human Services, November 5, 2019, https://www.hhs.gov/answers/hhs-administrative/what-programs-use-the -poverty-guidelines/index.html.

45   See author's calculation at www.lisep.org/mismeasurement.

46   Dave Kamper and Sebastian Martinez Hickey, "Tying Minimum-Wage Increases to Inflation, as 13 States Do, Will Lift Up Low-Wage Workers and Their Families across the Country," Economic Policy Institute, September 6, 2022, https://www.epi.org /blog/tying-minimum-wage-increases-to-inflation-as-12-states-do-will-lift-up-low -wage-workers-and-their-families-across-the-country/.

47   "Ohio Minimum Wage to Increase in 2024," Ohio Department of Commerce, September 29, 2023, https://com.ohio.gov/about-us/media-center/news/ohio -minimum-wage-to-increase-in-2024#:~:text=Thepercent20statepercent20minimumper cent20wagepercent20is,31percent2Cpercent202023.

48   Unions serve as a good example of how wages are directly tied to CPI as a measure of cost of living, because the agreements between employers and unions are public. Further, other contracts in the private sector may have wages or salaries indexed to the CPI although these are not public, and the general understanding of the level of inflation can influence negotiations between employers and employees to update compensation. Union collective bargaining agreements that include COLAs indexed to the CPI-W include those that have been negotiated by the Teamsters and UPS, United

Auto Workers and John Deere, Communications Workers of America and AT&T, and American Postal Workers Union and USPS. "UPS Teamsters to Receive $0.82 COLA Increase," International Brotherhood of Teamsters, accessed February 9, 2025, https ://teamster.org/2022/06/ups-teamsters-to-receive-0-82-cola-increase/; "Our Commitment," John Deere, accessed February 9, 2025, https://www.deere.com/assets /images/common/our-company/our-commitments.pdf?adobe_mc=TS%3D1740 607865%7CMCMID%3D61864096827730985530506610532817185810%7CMC ORGID%3D8CC867C25245ADC30A490D4C%2540AdobeOrg; "Groundbreaking! Tentative Agreement Reached with AT&T Mobility," CWA Union, accessed February 9, 2025, https://cwa-union.org/sites/default/files/20220627_att_mobility_ta.pdf; "Fourth COLA Announced: Pay Will Increase by $0.48 an Hour for Career Workers," American Postal Workers Union, August 10, 2023, https://apwu.org/news/colas-pay -information-pay/fourth-cola-announced.

49   Lydia Saad, "Historically Low Faith in US Institutions Continues," Gallup, July 6, 2023, https://news.gallup.com/poll/508169/historically-low-faith-institutions-continues.aspx.

Chapter 4

1   In 1950, manufacturing employment was 14.013 million and total nonfarm employment was 45.287 million according to the Current Employment Statistics Survey, so manufacturing made up 14.013/45.287 = 30.9 percent of nonfarm payrolls. In 2023, manufacturing accounted for 8.3 percent of total nonfarm employment with 12.940 million compared to 156.051 million for total nonfarm employment. "All Employees, Total Nonfarm [PAYNSA]," May 30, 2024, BLS via Federal Reserve Bank of St. Louis, https://fred.stlouisfed.org/series/PAYNSA; "U.S. Bureau of Labor Statistics, All Employees, Manufacturing [CEU3000000001]," BLS via Federal Reserve Bank of St. Louis, May 20, 2024, https://fred.stlouisfed.org/series/CEU3000000001.

2   Mehrsa Baradaran, *The Color of Money: Black Banks and the Racial Wealth Gap* (The Belknap Press of Harvard University Press, 2017), 106–133.

3   Jonny Dymond, "The Decline of US Manufacturing Jobs and Living Standards," BBC News, August 9, 2012, https://www.bbc.com/news/world-us-canada-18992241.

4   T. D. Snyder, ed., *120 Years of American Education: A Statistical Portrait* (US Department of Education, Office of Educational Research and Improvement, National Center for Education Statistics, 1993), 7 (Figure 2).

5   Todd Henneman, "Talkin' About Their Generations: The Workforce of the '50s and Today," Workforce.com, March 15, 2012, https://workforce.com/news/talkin-about -their-generations-the-workforce-of-the-50s-and-today.

6   Marvin Lazerson, "The Disappointments of Success: Higher Education after World War II," *The Annals of the American Academy of Political and Social Science* 559 (1998): 64–76, http://www.jstor.org/stable/1049607.

7   Raj Chetty et al., "The Fading American Dream: Trends in Absolute Income Mobility Since 1940," Opportunity Insights, accessed February 26, 2025, https://opportunity insights.org/paper/the-fading-american-dream/.

8   John F. Kennedy, "Excerpts From Annual Message to the Congress: The Economic
    Report of the President," The American Presidency Project, January 21, 1963, https
    ://www.presidency.ucsb.edu/documents/excerpts-from-annual-message-the-congress
    -the-economic-report-the-president#:~:text=1percent20dopercent20notpercent20expect
    percent20a,forpercent20taxpercent20reductionpercent20andpercent20reform.

9   *Britannica Money*, "Gross National Product," accessed February 10, 2025, https
    ://www.britannica.com/money/gross-national-product; "Real Gross National Product
    (GNPC96)," US Bureau of Economic Analysis via Federal Reserve Bank of St. Louis,
    May 30, 2024, https://fred.stlouisfed.org/series/GNPC96.

10 "The 1950s," History.com, updated June 18, 2024, https://www.history.com/topics
    /cold-war/1950s.

11 John F. Kennedy, "Remarks in Pueblo, Colorado Following Approval of the Fryingpan-
    Arkansas Project," The American Presidency Project, August 17, 1962, https://www
    .presidency.ucsb.edu/documents/remarks-pueblo-colorado-following-approval-the
    -fryingpan-arkansas-project.

12 These calculations, done in real terms, used the share of pretax national income for the
    bottom 50 percent and the top 1 percent as well as the pretax average income of the
    bottom 50 percent and top 5 percent among equal-split adults in the United States,
    using a custom dataset from the World Inequality Database (WID, https://wid.world
    /country/usa/), accessed May 6, 2024. The WID data for the United States is
    sourced from the Distributional National Accounts developed by Thomas Piketty,
    Emmanuel Saez, and Gabriel Zucman. See Thomas Piketty et al., "Distributional
    National Accounts: Methods and Estimates for the United States," *Quarterly Journal of
    Economics* 133, no. 2 (2018), 553–609.

13 These calculations used the CPI-U obtained from "Consumer Price Index for All Urban
    Consumers: All Items in US City Average (CPIAUCSL)," BLS via Federal Reserve
    Bank of St. Louis, May 23, 2024, https://fred.stlouisfed.org/series/CPIAUCSL. The
    raw weekly earnings measures for 1951, for the specific occupations "Durable Goods
    Manufacturing," "Special Trade Contractors," and "Food and Liquor Stores, Excluding
    Restaurants," were taken from Table SC-1 in US Bureau of Labor Statistics, *Employment
    and Earnings* (May 1954), https://fraser.stlouisfed.org/files/docs/publications
    /employment/emp_195405.pdf?utm_source=direct_download. For the usual weekly
    earnings for 1979, we use the December numbers for the specific occupations "Durable
    Goods Manufacturing," "Special Trade Contractors," and "Grocery Stores," from Table
    C-2 in US Bureau of Labor Statistics, *Employment and Earnings* 27, no. 1 (January
    1980), https://fraser.stlouisfed.org/files/docs/publications/employment/1980s/empl
    _011980.pdf?utm_source=direct_download.

14 Calculations used the annual median for "Lawyers with Some Experience." US Bureau
    of Labor Statistics, *Occupational Outlook Handbook* (1968–1969), HathiTrust, https
    ://babel.hathitrust.org/cgi/pt?id=osu.32435051428092&seq=233.

15   Median lawyer pay is likely understated relative to the pay in 1966 because this is a total figure (including lawyers with no and some experience) whereas the 1966 figure was for lawyers with some experience only. US Bureau of Labor Statistics, *Occupational Outlook Handbook* (accessed February 10, 2025), https://www.bls.gov/ooh/legal/lawyers.htm.

16   See BLS, *Occupational Outlook Handbook* (1968–1969), https://babel.hathitrust.org/cgi/pt?id=osu.32435051428092&seq=595. Page 595 compares workers in auto production with all production workers in manufacturing, so LISEP takes the $111.91 per week and multiplies that by 52.

17   Occupational Employment and Wage Statistics (OEWS) production workers in manufacturing industry. OEWS data for 2023 annual wages uses the same fifty-two-week assumption that was used in the 1966 comparison. BLS, *Occupational Outlook Handbook* (1968–1969).

18   BLS, *Occupational Outlook Handbook* (1968–1969), https://babel.hathitrust.org/cgi/pt?id=osu.32435051428092&seq=429. Page 409 provides the estimated average straight-time hourly earnings of skilled automobile mechanics at $3.81 in 1966. To annualize the hourly earnings, LISEP assumes a forty-hour workweek for fifty-two weeks in the year.

19   Occupation: Automotive Service Technicians and Mechanics (SOC code 493023), from OEWS 2023. Accessed on May 24, 2024. https://www.bls.gov/oes/current/oes493023.htm.

20   Specifically, this refers to "granted" compensation rather than "realized" compensation. The Economic Policy Institute's analysis provides both measures. The "granted" compensation measures the value of stock awards and options at the time when they are given rather than at the time when they are "realized" (meaning when the awards are vested and options are cashed in). Lawrence Mishel and Jori Kandra, "CEO Pay Has Skyrocketed 1,322% since 1978," Economic Policy Institute, August 10, 2021, https://www.epi.org/publication/ceo-pay-in-2020/.

21   This number refers to the "granted" compensation rather than "realized" compensation. Mishel and Kandra, "CEO Pay Has Skyrocketed 1,322%."

22   Raj Chetty et al., "The Fading American Dream: Trends in Absolute Income Mobility Since 1940," 398–406.

23   "Real Gross Domestic Product Per Capita (A939RX0Q048SBEA)," BLS via Federal Reserve Bank of St. Louis, May 23, 2024, https://fred.stlouisfed.org/series/A939RX0Q048SBEA.

24   This argument is made powerfully in many books, including Philipp Lepenies, *The Power of a Single Number: A Political History of GDP* (Columbia University Press, 2016); Diane Coyle, *GDP: A Brief but Affectionate History* (Princeton University Press, 2015); Mariana Mazzucato, *The Value of Everything: Making and Taking in the Global Economy* (PublicAffairs, 2018).

25   Aaron Zitner, "Voters See American Dream Slipping Out of Reach, WSJ/NORC Poll Shows," *The Wall Street Journal*, November 24, 2023, https://www.wsj.com/us-news/american-dream-out-of-reach-poll-3b774892?mod=hp_lead_pos1.

26   Estelle Sommeiller et al., "Income Inequality in the US by State, Metropolitan Area, and County," Economic Policy Institute, June 16, 2016, https://www.epi.org/public ation/income-inequality-in-the-us/.

27   Signe-Mary McKernan et al., "Wealth Inequalities," Urban Institute, September 2015, https://www.urban.org/policy-centers/cross-center-initiatives/inequality-and-mobility /projects/wealth-inequalities.

28   *Life at the End of the Century* (Pew Research Center, July 3, 1999), https://www.pew research.org/politics/1999/07/03/life-at-the-end-of-the-century/.

29   Alexandre Tanzi, "More Than Half of Middle-Income Americans Are Downbeat on Their Finances," Bloomberg, October 12, 2023, https://www.bloomberg.com/news /articles/2023-10-12/more-than-half-of-middle-income-us-households-are-downbeat -about-their-finances?leadSource=uverifypercent20wall&embedded-checkout=true.

30   According to author's calculation of Shared Economic Prosperity metric. Specifically, disposable income rose by 57.4 percent for the top 1 percent of earners from 2001 to 2023, adjusted using the CPI-U; it increased 4.7 percent and 8.5 percent for the middle 60 percent and bottom 60 percent, respectively, adjusted using LISEP's Minimal Quality of Life index.

31   Young Jo and Ilya Rahkovsky, "Higher Incomes and Greater Time Constraints Lead to Purchasing More Convenience Foods," US Department of Agriculture Economic Resource Service, June 27, 2018, www.ers.usda.gov/amber-waves/2018/june/higher -incomes-and-greater-time-constraints-lead-to-purchasing-more-convenience-foods.

32   For more thorough explanations and rationale for the importance of these goods, see lisep.org/mql.

33   "Real Gross Domestic Product (GDPC1)," BEA via Federal Reserve Bank of St. Louis, accessed May 23, 2024, https://fred.stlouisfed.org/series/GDPC1; "Real Gross Domestic Product Per Capita (A939RX0Q048SBEA)," BEA via Federal Reserve Bank of St. Louis.

34   See lisep.org/sep for calculations.

35   Although it might seem odd that neither the bottom 60 percent nor the top 40 percent have a growth rate of at least GDP per capita, this is not an error. There are several reasons that GDP per capita would exceed disposable income, but the most important for our analysis is the use of the deflator for GDP per capita. Although GDP per capita is meant to convey the well-being of each citizen, instead of using even the inflation rate faced by the average person (as measured in CPI-U), it uses the GDP deflator—a blend of adjustments for prices faced by consumers (using the PCE), prices faced by producers (using the Produce Price Index, or PPI), and prices faced in international trade (using Import-Export Price Indexes, or MXPIs,). Thomas Blanchet et al., "Real-time Inequality," Working Paper No. 30229 (National Bureau of Economic Research, revised November 2022), 9, https://www.nber.org/system/files/working_papers/ w30229/w30229.pdf; "BEA publishes several inflation measures; which should I use?," US Bureau of Economic Analysis, updated October 25, 2018, https://www.bea.gov /help/faq/509; "The Role of BLS Import and Export Price Indexes in the Real GDP," *Monthly Labor Review*, June 2015, https://www.bls.gov/opub/mlr/2015/article/the-role -of-bls-import-and-export-price-indexes-in-the-real-gdp.htm#_edn14.

36   "More Than 53 Million People Received Help from Food Banks and Food Pantries in
     2021," Feeding America, June 15, 2022, https://www.feedingamerica.org/about
     -us/press-room/53-million-received-help-2021#:~:text=Thepercent20reportpercent20fi
     ndspercent20thatpercent20more,thanpercent20priorpercent20topercent20the
     percent20pandemic.

37   Megan Brenan, "Record High in US Put Off Medical Care Due to Cost in 2022,"
     Gallup, February 6, 2023, news.gallup.com/poll/468053/record-high-put-off-medical
     -care-due-to-cost-2022.aspx#:~:text=Apercent20newpercent20highpercent20of
     percent2035,andpercent20olderpercent20saidpercent20thepercent20same.

38   Daniel Soucy et al., *State of Homelessness: 2023 Edition* (National Alliance to End
     Homelessness, 2023), https://endhomelessness.org/wp-content/uploads/2024/08
     /StateOfHomelessness_2023.pdf.

39   Richard Fry et al., "A Majority of Young Adults in the US Live with Their Parents for
     the First Time since the Great Depression," Pew Research Center, September 9, 2020,
     www.pewresearch.org/short-reads/2020/09/04/a-majority-of-young-adults-in-the-u-s
     -live-with-their-parents-for-the-first-time-since-the-great-depression/.

40   Calculations are based on the ACS survey. LISEP takes households where all earners
     are in their thirties and then compares the median-wage income per hour in total. To
     get the median of the different percentiles, for example, we take the upper 10 percent
     as measured by total income (*not* the hourly income) of households with the head(s) of
     households in their thirties, and then calculate the median hourly income of this subset
     of the population. See www.lisep.org/mismeasurement for more details.

41   The series come from the Current Employment Statistics establishment survey. Annual
     averages by super sector. "All Employees, Manufacturing (MANEMP)," BLS via Federal
     Reserve Bank of St. Louis, accessed February 26, 2025, https://fred.stlouisfed.org/series
     /MANEMP; "All Employees, Retail Trade (USTRADE)," BLS via Federal Reserve Bank
     of St. Louis, accessed February 26, 2025, https://fred.stlouisfed.org/series/USTRADE;
     "All Employees, Leisure and Hospitality (USLAH)," BLS via Federal Reserve Bank of
     St. Louis, accessed February 26, 2025, https://fred.stlouisfed.org/series/USLAH.

42   Data are from "Current Population Survey Data for Social, Economic and Health
     Research," IPUMS CPS, accessed December 15, 2023, https://cps.ipums.org. LISEP
     uses the ASEC sample, then defines wages according to IPUMS CPS: as "each
     respondent's total pre-tax wage and salary income . . . reported for the previous calendar
     year" ("INWAGE: Description," accessed February 10, 2024, https://cps.ipums.org/cps
     -action/variables/INCWAGE#description_section) for employees and incorporated self-
     employed workers, or as "each respondent's net pre-income-tax non-farm business and/
     or professional practice income reported for the previous calendar year" ("INCBUS:
     Description," accessed February 10, 2024, https://cps.ipums.org/cps-action/variables
     /INCBUS#description_section) for unincorporated self-employed workers. Workers
     are assumed to be either self-employed or employees, as the self-employment criterion
     corresponds to the job held longest during the prior year. Wages are then adjusted
     to January 2024 dollars using the CPI-U, and wage percentiles are determined for
     individuals within each occupation, including both self-employed and employees. See
     www.lisep.org/mismeasurement for more details.

43   Urban Institute WorkRise fellow Elisabeth Jacobs describes the middle class as "running to stand still." Ashleigh Maciolek and Hannah Van Drie, "Monitoring the Middle Class: How the American Middle Class Is Really Doing," Brookings Institution, February 11, 2021, https://www.brookings.edu/articles/monitoring-the-middle-class-how-the-american-middle-class-is-really-doing/.

44   The only meaningful progress for the middle class seems to come from the rising efforts of working women: "We estimate that if women's average earnings dropped back to their 1979 levels, average middle-class family incomes would have grown by only 22 percent between 1979 and 2018. . . . Average family income actually grew by 211 percent over this period." Isabel V. Sawhill and Katherine Guyot, *The Middle Class Time Squeeze* (Brookings Institution, August 2020), 17, 20, https://www.brookings.edu/wp-content/uploads/2020/08/The-Middle-Class-Time-Squeeze_08.18.2020.pdf.

45   Daniel de Visé, "The Top 1% of American Earners Now Own More Wealth Than the Entire Middle Class," *USA Today*, December 6, 2023, https://www.usatoday.com/story/money/2023/12/06/top-1-american-earners-more-wealth-middle-class/71769832007/.

46   "History of US Homeownership: How Housing Has Changed since 1960," The Zebra, March 13, 2024, https://www.thezebra.com/resources/home/housing-trends-visualized/#:~:text=Thepercent20medianpercent20housepercent20ofpercent201960,inpercent201960percent20topercent20percent2468percent2C703percent20today.

47   "Homeownership Rate," Brookings Institute, accessed February 10, 2025, https://www.brookings.edu/articles/the-middle-class-monitor/?section=homeownership.

48   "Minimal Quality of Life," Ludwig Institute for Shared Economic Prosperity, accessed February 10, 2025, https://www.lisep.org/mql.

49   Brenan, "Record High in US Put Off Medical Care."

50   Author's calculations are based on the total disposable income and the share remaining of the top 40 percent if MQL for the bottom 60 percent were achieved in 2023.

Conclusion

1   "Direction of the United States," YouGov, accessed February 10, 2025, https://today.yougov.com/topics/politics/trackers/direction-of-the-united-states.

2   Matthew F. Garnett and Sally C. Curtin, "Suicide Mortality in the United States, 2001–2021," NCHS Data Brief No. 464, National Center for Health Statistics, April 2023, https://www.cdc.gov/nchs/products/databriefs/db464.htm; "Life Expectancy in the U.S. Dropped for the Second Year in a Row in 2021," National Center for Health Statistics, August 31, 2022, https://www.cdc.gov/nchs/pressroom/nchs_press_releases/2022/20220831.htm.

3   Robin Lake and Travis Pillow, "The Alarming State of the American Student in 2022," Brookings Institution, November 1, 2022, https://www.brookings.edu/articles/the-alarming-state-of-the-american-student-in-2022/; "Do US Parents Overestimate Their Students' Progress?," National Center on Education and the Economy, January 14, 2021, https://ncee.org/quick-read/do-u-s-parents-overestimate-their-students-progress/.

4   "The Most Alarming Trends in Drug Use Demographics Over the Last 5 Years,"
      PharmChek, April 27, 2023, https://www.pharmchek.com/resources/blog/the-most
      -alarming-trends-in-drug-use-demographics-over-the-last-5-years.

5   Olivia Ferrari, "Private Jets Are Increasingly Replacing Car Trips—for the Ultra-Wealthy,"
      National Geographic, November 7, 2024, https://www.nationalgeographic.com/environ
      ment/article/private-jet-flights-climate-change.

Index

About the Author

Gene Ludwig, 27th comptroller of the currency, is a business and civic leader and expert on banking, regulation, risk management, and fiscal policy. He has been the vice chairman and senior control officer of one of the largest banks in America and the founder of successful financial technology companies. He was also an instigator of the modern Community Reinvestment Act, worked toward the effective enforcement of our anti-discrimination laws, and championed the creation of the Community Development Financial Institution sector. In 2019, he founded the Ludwig Institute for Shared Economic Prosperity (LISEP), a nonprofit dedicated to improving the economic well-being of low- and middle-income Americans through research and education.

His writing has appeared in *The New York Times*, *The Wall Street Journal*, *The Atlantic*, Politico, the *Financial Times*, and *TIME*. He holds a master's degree from Oxford University and a JD from Yale

University, where he was on the *Yale Law Journal* and chairman of Yale Legislative Services. He is the author of *The Vanishing American Dream* and *The Mismeasurement of America.*

About The Ludwig Institute for Shared Economic Prosperity

The Ludwig Institute for Shared Economic Prosperity (LISEP) produces original economic research to provide a more accurate picture of the well-being of middle- and lower-income households. Our research includes new economic indicators for both unemployment and earnings. Our statistics aim to provide policymakers and the public with a more transparent view into the economic situation of all Americans as compared with the traditionally relied upon metrics.

LISEP also seeks to guide and support policy initiatives that increase opportunities for struggling Americans, including initiatives dedicated to determining how we can create a business environment that supports good-paying jobs.

Learn more at www.lisep.org.

The following is an excerpt from Gene Ludwig's 2020 book
*The Vanishing American Dream: A Frank Look at the Economic
Realities Facing Middle- and Lower-Income Americans.*

Disruption Books | Hardcover: 978-1-63331-044-5
Paperback: 978-1-63331-063-6 | eBook: 978-1-63331-045-2

Second Panel

What can be done at the national level to boost the economic well-being of middle- and lower-income Americans?

If the first panel was framed by Admiral Stockdale's quote from the 1992 presidential debate, the second panel was framed by a quote Andrew Tisch included in his remarks: the classic line from the Howard Beale character in the movie *Network*: "I'm mad as hell, and I'm not going to take this anymore!" Participants articulated a wide range of theories as to what might be changed nationally to help middle- and working-class Americans climb the ladder of prosperity. And interestingly enough, for all the vigor in the debate, reform ideas were focused not on any one social injustice, but on ways to expand opportunity across a whole range of sectors.

The sheer breadth of the discussion was remarkable. Panelists lobbed in ideas for national-scale solutions that ranged from higher education to unpaid work, and from infrastructure prioritization to smart regulation. Striking throughout the discussion was the sense that education has become an almost indispensable ticket to middle-class life. Education has always been a leg up—but during the Industrial Era, you could thrive without a high school degree. Today, by contrast, that's rarely the case. With that underlying reality in mind, most proposals sought either to (a) provide more Americans with the skills they need or (b) help those struggling without the benefit of such credentials to improve their condition.

Certainly, as nearly everyone agreed, the circumstances have become more dire in many parts of the country. But unmistakable throughout the discussion was a sense that policymakers and private/nonprofit-sector leaders still have cards to play. Certain challenges in public life may simply be too big for any institution to tackle. But here, in one room, were experts with a plethora of proposals that could and should be tried. Easy as it may have been to come away from the first panel with your head in your hands, the second panel highlighted a variety of potential action items that provide us at least some sense of optimism.

ɑ

LAWRENCE H. SUMMERS, *Charles W. Eliot University Professor and President Emeritus, Harvard University; Former Secretary, US Treasury Department; and Former Director, National Economic Council:* Our first speaker is Andy Tisch, who has been a leader in terms of business thoughtfulness and has given a lot of thought to these issues around the responsibility of business. His corporation has tried in ways consistent with business values to do a variety of things to make the world a better place.

ANDREW TISCH, *Co-chairman of the Board and Chairman of the Executive Committee, Loews Corporation:* Let me open with a quote that may be familiar to many of you. "We know things are bad—worse than bad. They're crazy. It's like everything, everywhere, is going crazy, so we don't go out anymore. We sit in the house, and slowly the world we are living in is getting smaller, and all we say is, 'Please, at least leave us alone in our living rooms.'" Now, the speaker of that quote is Howard Beale, and the movie is *Network*. Though it was released forty-three years ago, Paddy Chayefsky's words feel just as relevant today.

So many of our fellow citizens, especially those in the beleaguered middle class, share Howard Beale's feelings of anger and alienation. What does it mean to be in the middle class? It depends on whom you ask. It depends on where they live. It depends on how much money they make. It depends on a lot of things. But in many ways, middle class is really a state of mind.

I recall being in China—probably ten years ago, specifically on a Friday night, specifically in Xi'an. It was December 24, Christmas Eve, and we were going across town to go to dinner. I witnessed probably a half a million young Chinese men and women partying—subzero temperatures, everyone there celebrating, no inebriation, no intoxication. What were they celebrating? Who knew? Who cared? Our host said it was the new Chinese middle class, celebrating the fact that every year since their birth, they had seen their quality of life improve by 7 percent to 9 percent.

We certainly do not see that euphoria in our middle class. Decades ago, the middle-class mindset was defined by aspiration, by a belief that if you worked hard, you could buy a home, support your family, send your kids to a good school—and you could do it on one salary. It was called the American Dream. Today, the middle-class aspiration has curdled into anxiety.

All this as wages stagnate and both spouses go to work. The basic costs of living have spiraled upward. Family health insurance premiums and housing costs are growing twice as fast as workers' earnings. The cost of attending a four-year public school has tripled in the past thirty years.

While this has happened, the ratio of CEO pay to that of the average worker has grown from 30 to 1, in 1978, to 270 to 1 today. Is it any wonder that middle-class people are getting mad as hell and they're not going to take it anymore? The dysfunction and polarization in our government are both a cause and a symptom of this anger, because Washington's decisions and indecision have played a direct role in the decline of America's once-great middle class. It's a symptom because angry citizens are electing angrier and more intolerant candidates who see compromise as a form of treason. The vicious cycle is continuing; the middle class feels unwanted, unprotected, unappreciated, unloved, and abandoned.

Why has income stagnated in the middle class? One of the reasons is that for the first time in our history, one can create a significant amount of wealth without assets—and sometimes without employees. You don't need pipelines, steel mills, factories, or legions of employees to build a great company. You just need an idea. Very few middle-class employees are needed to sustain wealth. Look at Amazon—600,000 employees at minimum or lower wages.

Look at General Motors. At its peak, General Motors employed 850,000 people worldwide, 600,000 of them in the United States. The two largest companies in the United States by market cap today are Microsoft and Apple. These two companies combined employ less than a third of the number of people that GM once did. America's leaders in government, business, and elsewhere still don't know what to do about it. For too long, too many leaders have focused exclusively on today with very little regard to tomorrow.

Politicians do what they need to do to get to the next election, which typically involves peddling simple slogans for complex problems, and trying to divide rather than to unite. Companies do what they can to get to the next quarter. It's real short-termism. This approach is failing not only this generation, but the ones to come.

In business, there is a line item in every company's budget called maintenance capex. Now, capital expenditures for maintenance aren't sexy. When a company's finances are tight, they're the easiest to cut because the cost of deferral does not show up immediately—that is, until your ship turns into a rusting hunk of metal or the assembly line breaks down completely. Then the bill comes due, and it's usually much more expensive than it would have been if you paid for everything on time. Well, the bill is coming due for America's middle class. The bill for our future is coming due because of our failure to rebuild infrastructure . . . to invest in education . . . to properly fund Medicare, Medicaid, and Social Security. Trillion-dollar deficits as far out as the eye can see. It's just like businesses endlessly deferring their maintenance capex, and the bill is coming, which is why Gene has asked us all here today.

When Howard Beale made his primal scream forty-three years ago, it felt to many as if America was in a permanent decline. We were not. We rationalized our businesses. We rewrote our tax codes. We right-sized our federal budget to the point where we eliminated our national debt. Leaders in business and government made bold reforms, and American ingenuity was released to tackle the previously intractable problems.

What we need to do now is get mad as hell and not take it anymore.

SUMMERS: Bob Shiller has won the Nobel Prize in economics. What stands out about Bob again and again is his way of having a different idiosyncratic and successful slant on a whole range of economic issues—most famously, on the once-fashionable idea that markets are rational arbiters of value. This idea is held in much less repute today than it once was, because of—more than any other person—Bob and his work.

ROBERT SHILLER, *Professor of Economics, Yale University, and Nobel Laureate*: I am going to list some of the insurance- and finance-related efforts to deal with inequality. I was inspired by the work of Gustav von Schmoller, an economist in Germany in the nineteenth century. Around 1900, he wrote in his memoirs *Character Builders* that the nineteenth century was a great period for the expansion and application of the concept of insurance to problems facing society. He and others led the way for Germany adopting the first social security system, the first accident insurance, the first government-sponsored health insurance system, under [statesman Otto von] Bismarck. It wasn't Bismarck—it was the economists who did this. The important thing about carefully constructed insurance contracts is that they can help you avoid gratuitous inequality. We're not interested in taking the money away from a family that became a millionaire family by working fourteen-hour days in the family store for a lifetime. That's not what we want to take away. We want to take away that random, senseless part of inequality.

I wrote a book, *Macro Markets*, in 1993, about how financial markets can deal with risk to people or directly, and another one, *New Financial Order*, in 2003, and then *Finance and the Good Society*. I'm doing a very quick summary. History encourages me to think that these ideas are slow to develop. I don't get easily discouraged when people don't jump on these ideas. We still don't have national health insurance; that's over a century-long effort. The first principle I want to mention is what I call in my books "livelihood insurance." It could be privately offered, but the idea is that we want people to ensure their careers. When you get a Yale law degree, you could develop an insurance against people who get similar degrees showing a decline in lifetime earnings. This could help you reeducate yourself and make a transition, if it works out badly. Yale Law School does this already with the Koch program, but it's not done widely. This is another example of how slowly these things happen.

Another one is home equity insurance, which there have been several attempts to start. This hasn't been a success. But the idea is that your home might lose value, and that's the majority of most people's wealth. So, it should be protected. You buy an insurance policy—it could be in addition to your homeowners insurance policy—that ensures you against declines in the price of homes; a major protection against inequality. In the process [of writing these books], I did manage to succeed somewhat in establishing a futures market for a single-family home.

[The late economist] Karl Case and I created home-price indices that were specifically designed to be the settlement basis for contracts on home prices. In 2006, the Chicago Mercantile Exchange created markets for ten US cities, including New York and Boston, which are still going today.

Again, however, it's disappointing—it hasn't developed into a major market. But it is predicting a weakening of the housing market. Also, the options markets on single-family homes—we succeeded in getting that started, but it hasn't attracted attention. It's a very weak market. I don't get discouraged for the long term, because I think the real problem is there. It's going to happen to homes on the coasts when the sea level rises, if it does from climate change, and there's no plan in place to help people.

I just mentioned health insurance. That's not one of my innovations, but it's something that goes back to Germany in the late nineteenth century. It is an amazing development of modern civilization. Another invention—it's not mine, but I'm putting it on my list—is long-term property and casualty insurance. Right now, your homeowners insurance will adjust your rates as conditions change, but things happen to homes in [certain] regions. I mentioned global warming, but it's also things like hurricanes. There's nothing in your homeowners insurance policy to protect you against the possibility that there will be a whole new era of massive hurricanes destroying homes.

The critical point about the insurance of our time is that you have to deal with it before it happens. Let me also mention inequality insurance—insurance against rising inequality—which will be in our government program. It would be a plan to raise taxes in the future on the rich, if inequality gets even worse than it is today. I think that is more likely to succeed than doing it now. This is also [lawyer and economist] Ian Ayres's idea here at the Yale Law School—I call them "continuous workout mortgages." They have a preplanned workout. In the last financial crisis, we discovered that nothing was planned for all these people whose home price declined massively and who now have a debt greater than their home value. We should have mortgages that take this into account in advance.

Finally, international risk management—I'm surprised there is not much talk at all about what we will do if global warming requires massive migrations from one hard-hit region to another. There has to be a plan, some kind of risk-sharing across nations.

SUMMERS: The next speaker is Daniel Markovits, who has written proactively on a whole variety of aspects of law and public philosophy, and whom I have found most interesting as a critic of meritocracy.

DANIEL MARKOVITS, *Professor of Law, Yale Law School:*
I want to start by fixing a particular account of the problem. In any economy, there are two kinds of inequality. There's low-end inequality, which concerns the gap between the poor and the middle class, and there's high-end inequality, which concerns the gap between the middle class and the rich. Historically in this country—when LBJ's Great Society got going, for example—the core problem was low-end inequality.

Today, the core problem is high-end inequality. You can see that the share of national income captured by the top 1 percent has roughly doubled in the past fifty years, even as the poverty rate as conventionally measured has fallen to between a half and a quarter of what it was at the middle of the Great Recession. You can also see, if you look at Gini coefficients, something extraordinarily striking. Separating out Ginis within the bottom 70 percent of the income distribution and within the top 5 percent reveals that inequality in the bottom 70 percent remains lower than it was in 1964, while inequality within the top 5 percent has skyrocketed. Indeed, there have been recent years in which the Gini within the top 5 percent has exceeded the Gini for the entire income distribution. So there is now more income inequality in the richest twentieth of the US population than in the population as a whole, which tells you how concentrated income has become at the top.

Moreover, the rich now distinctively work. Probably three-quarters of the increase in the top 1 percent share of national income over the past fifty years is attributable not to a shift away from labor and toward capital but rather to a shift within labor—from mid-skilled, middle-class labor to super-skilled, super-elite labor. The elite gets this income by working long, long hours. Among full-time, non-self-employed, prime-aged men, the bottom 60 percent of the income distribution now work nearly 20 percent fewer hours per week than they did in 1940. The top 1 percent now work about 15 percent more hours. In absolute terms, this is a shift of the labor effort away from the typical bottom-half worker to the typical top 1 percent worker of sixteen hours a week, or two regulation workdays.

The phenomena that we were describing earlier, importantly including technological change, are suppressing opportunities for middle-class work to a degree that approaches the extent to which gender discrimination suppressed women's opportunities for market work at mid-twentieth century. We therefore face maldistribution that distinctively concerns not poverty but rather wealth.

This story of how we got here focuses on a massive and historically unprecedented concentration of human capital—in particular, education and training—in a very, very narrow elite that is increasingly chosen on account of being children of rich parents.

To begin with, college graduates are marrying each other as they never did in the past and at such rates that there are very few college graduates left over to marry people who didn't graduate from college.

Next, education increasingly influences parenting. Historically, the chances of having a child outside of marriage were largely not determined by a person's education. Today, the bottom two-thirds of the distribution by education have over half their children outside of marriage. The richest 5 percent not only bear children within marriage, but they raise their children almost entirely within intact, stable marriages. These families then spend enormous amounts of resources on educating their children outside of school. The gap between top-quintile and bottom-quintile enrichment expenditures has tripled in the past thirty years. Within school, the gaps are even greater: The gap between a typical middle-class family's school education expenditure per child and a typical poor family's [expenditure] is roughly $5,000 a year. But the gap between a middle-class family's and an elite family's [expenditures] can reach $60,000 a year.

This produces massive differences in childhood achievement. Academic achievement, as measured by school testing, for middle-class and poor children has been roughly stable or even convergent over the past fifty years, even as rich children outstrip middle-class ones, in patterns that closely mirror income ratios. Moreover, these are very, very large effects. For example, by 2000, the rich/poor achievement gap had come to exceed what the white/black gap was in 1954, which is the year *Brown v. Board of Education* was decided. Economic inequality is producing differences in educational achievement today in the United States as great as apartheid did at midcentury. Moreover, the gaps again are principally rich/middle class gaps, not middle class/poor gaps.

These gaps endure as children grow up. On the SAT, the gap between the average score of a child whose parents make over $200,000 a year and [that of] a child whose parents make between $40,000 and $60,000 is twice as big as the gap between a middle-class child and a child at or below the poverty line. This produces the skewed elite. A child's odds of going to college and the quality of the college that the child attends both rise steadily alongside parental income rank.

At the most elite colleges, the skew to wealth is even greater. At the 150 or so most competitive colleges, kids from the top quarter of the income distribution outweigh kids from the bottom quarter by 14 to 1, and—in a way, more strikingly—outweigh kids from each of the middle two quarters by about 6 to 1. At the Ivy Plus colleges, there are more kids from parents in the top 1 percent than in the bottom half. At the most elite tip of the Ivy Plus—Harvard, Princeton, Stanford, and Yale—there are more kids from the top 1 percent than from the bottom 60 percent.

One way to think about this is to compare this way of transmitting privilege to the traditional aristocratic way, which was to give bequests of physical or financial capital to children on the death of their parents. Imagine that each year, you took the difference between what a typical 1 percent household spends on educating its children and what a typical middle-class family spends, and you put that into the S&P 500 and then gave it as a bequest to the child on the death of the parents. That would yield roughly $10 million per child. That's the extent of the intergenerational transmission of advantage through the mechanism of accumulated human capital.

Why do people do it? It is mainly that education has such enormously high social and economic returns today. Whereas there was basically no professional school premium or graduate school premium to wages in 1970, today someone without a high school degree has only about a 1-in-75 chance of earning as much over her lifetime as the median professional school graduate. Somebody with only a high school degree—that's roughly two-thirds of the population—has only a 1-in-40 chance of earning as much. Someone with only a BA has only about a 1-in-6 chance of earning as much as the median professional school graduate.

If we're interested in a solution to such inequality, we need to dilute this human capital at the top—and massively open up education, including elite education, to the broad middle class.

SUMMERS: Thank you for a very powerful presentation. Our next speaker is Sarah Bloom Raskin, who most recently served as the deputy secretary of the Treasury. She has been involved in financial regulation and the protection of consumers in one way or another for a very long time.

SARAH BLOOM RASKIN, *Former Deputy Secretary, US Treasury Department, and Former Member, Federal Reserve Board*: I'm going to attempt to be super pragmatic. There are three things that we can be doing at the national level to deal with what has been laid out as significant deviations from optimal prosperity. First of all, I'm going to talk about improving our measurements. Second, I want to talk about investing in priorities that have the highest returns on investment (ROIs). Third, I want to say something about how we do it, which is by giving states and localities great latitude to run pilots that produce results, which can be then evaluated and scaled up.

First of all, in terms of improving our measurements, Gene has laid out an important challenge here—that our measurements are not really giving us a full understanding and a full way to communicate the extent of the issues that we're talking about. I want to point out two particular macrostatistics that need to be added to the lexicon.

One is a Jacob Hacker innovation, the Economic Security Index. This is an index that is going to take a lot of the pieces—which Andrea [Levere] laid out so well and which Gene has laid out—and capture them in a macroaggregate. While it is good to have an understanding of these granular pieces, I think that if we want a data point that's going to compete with the top headliners of the unemployment rate and GDP, I think we need a macrostatistic. I'm going to advocate for a statistic that captures some of the fragility in the lower- and middle-income parts of our country. This could be the Economic Security Index; there are other candidates for it, but something like that would be a good start.

The second data point is looking at unpaid work. This is looking at the labor done by unpaid workers and is currently not part of GDP. When I talk about unpaid work, what is this? In developing countries, a lot of times it's hauling the water; it can be quite physical.

In the United States it is taking care of sick family members, washing the dishes, transporting the kids, caring for elderly parents. These are measures of productivity that are not captured in any way. We should think about how to capture them. We've got some good hints that this could be useful. The Gates Foundation has found that reducing women's unpaid labor from five hours a day to three hours a day could increase a country's female labor force participation rate by 10 percent. Thinking about how we bring into our metrics an understanding of unpaid work is a useful area to pursue.

Second, we should consider investing in priorities that have a high ROI. In this example, what I am seeing is investments in human capital. How do we evaluate various investments in human capital? This is something that begins to turn positive results in terms of higher pay and better employment. For example, there's a 13 percent ROI for comprehensive, high-quality, birth-to-five-years-old early education. This is not the childhood education that is in the headlines, which is, what do we do in the elementary school years? I'm talking birth to five years old. What do we see? We are seeing improved health outcomes. We are seeing improved social behaviors, higher pay, better employment. And we're also seeing reduced cost coming later in terms of health care and costs associated with poverty. This research comes from [economist] James Heckman, and it focuses on the life-cycle benefits of an influential early childhood program geared to the ages zero to five.

A study was done in North Carolina of poor African American children from ages zero to five—one model with excellent nutrition, fantastic day care, support for working parents, and early learning, and another model with the current state of childcare in that state. Children were randomly assigned to either the higher-quality resources or the lower-quality resources. Data is collected longitudinally—data points are taken through to adulthood. What has been shown are positive effects on high school graduation; positive effects on years of education, adult employment, and lower drug use; lower blood pressure and better health outcomes; and higher labor income. We see a two-generational effect. For example, mothers can enter the workforce, and their earnings can go up because their children are gaining the foundational skills necessary to put the mother at ease—as well as to make the children, as they develop, more productive in a future workforce. This childcare generation absolutely generates very positive ROI.

Finally, we should be running these studies locally. We need to think about piloting some of this work at the state level. Then, with good pilots in hand, we can compare ROIs and make credible policy recommendations.

ZACH LISCOW, *Associate Professor of Law, Yale Law School*: I want to take up the question posed by Gene, of how to sort among these surfeit proposals for helping lower-income Americans. I want to return to intellectual foundations. We economic experts should cool it somewhat when it comes to finding the most efficient solutions, as conventionally defined, to addressing these problems.

I'll describe what I mean. Let me begin with an illustrative example on infrastructure spending. Many of us in the room think it is important. As has long been the practice—including under President Barack Obama—when the Department of Transportation allocates money to projects, it does cost-benefit analyses to find the most valuable projects. The key component in that analysis is the value of time saved in transit. The current practice by the Department of Transportation is to value the time of the poor less than the time of the rich.

As a result, if the Department of Transportation is comparing a project—say, a bus line to help lower-income people—it will value the time of people less and be less likely to fund the project than if it's considering a project in airports that will primarily benefit the rich. We have baked into our rules a system that will tend to push money toward the rich and away from the poor, at a time when you think it's really important that the poor be able to make it to work in order to achieve economic mobility. How could it possibly be that even in the Obama administration we had a rule like this? How could it possibly be that we treat the poor so much worse, given that they're the ones who really need the transportation spending?

There is a core economic logic to it, to having this practice, even if you care about helping the poor, which is that this is efficient. It is efficient to spend a lot less on the poor to get them to work than to spend on the rich. The basic logic is that the economic pie grows more if you get the richer person to work more quickly, because that richer person earns more wages per hour than a poor person will earn per hour. The efficient thing to do—even if you really care economically, even if you really care about the poor—is to spend lots and lots of money getting the rich to work more quickly, grow the size of the economic pie, and then give cash transfers to the poor. Use tax and transfers to make everyone better off.

This is the system. This is the economic logic that we're very familiar with. That's what we teach undergrads; that's what we teach law students. This is the logic of the elites. Yet this logic is problematic, and it's incomplete. It often hinders good policy analysis.